Kiac
4/18

LOOM
KNITTING
SOCKS

ISELA PHELPS

D1224253

LOOM
KNITTING
SOCKS

A Beginner's Guide to Knitting Socks
on a Loom with Over 50 Fun Projects

ISELA PHELPS

St. Martin's Griffin
New York

Loom Knitting Socks. Copyright © 2009 Quintet
Publishing Limited. All rights reserved.
QTT.LKS

For information, address
St. Martin's Press, 175 Fifth Avenue, New York
NY 10010

The written instructions, photographs, designs,
patterns, and projects in this volume are intended
for personal use of the reader and may be
reproduced for that purpose only.

www.stmartins.com

This book was designed and produced by
Quintet Publishing Limited, 6 Blundell Street
London N7 9BH, UK

Art Director: Michael Charles
Designer: Tania Field
Photography: Jonny Thompson
Illustrator: Anthony Duke, Bernard Chau
Project Editor: Martha Burley
Managing Editor: Donna Gregory
Publisher: James Tavendale

Printed in China by 1010 Printing International
Limited

Library of Congress Cataloging-in-Publication Data
Available Upon Request

ISBN: 978-0-312-58998-1

First Edition: October 2009

10 9 8 7 6 5 4 3 2 1

Contents

Introduction

The joy of socks

Socks are dear to my heart! From the instant I learned to loom knit, I knew that socks would be my number one project. They are simply amazing to create. Each time I make one, I feel that I have created magic. It all starts just like a hat, a simple tube, then you begin knitting a flat panel and you incorporate a few short rows. Miraculously this creates a small perfect cup to fit your heel, and as you continue knitting the tube and repeating the short-row process, another cup is formed for the toes. Magic!

Socks are the perfect project to have around. They are small, which makes them portable, and if you have a few going at all times, monotony keeps at bay. I can pack one with me whenever I am running errands and waiting at appointments. Socks—portable, fun, and easy!

Isela Phelps

How to use this book

This book is designed to be an easy source of reference and inspiration. The first chapter has step-by-step illustrations which guide you through the many stitches and design elements that are vital in creating your socks.

For real inspiration, the 50 projects that follow this introduction vary in technique, size, expertise, and challenge.

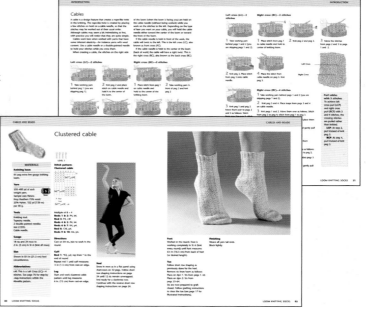

Pattern style in this book

The patterns in the book are written in a short format to save on space and may have unfamiliar syntax. Here is an example:

Short version:
CO 24sts, join to work in the round.
Work in 2x2 Rib stitch for 1 in. (2.5 cm).
Work in St st. until leg measures 6 in. (15 cm) from CO edge.

Long version:
Cast on 24 stitches/pegs. Connect the last stitch to the first stitch to prepare to knit in rounds.
Knit 2 stitches/pegs, purl 2 stitches/pegs, repeat the sequence around the loom until you reach the end of the round. Repeat the entire sequence until you have 1 inch (2.5 cm) of work.
Switch to stockinette stitch (knit all rounds) and knit until you reach 6 inches (15 cm) from the cast-on edge.

Pattern punctuation

*: used to mark the beginning of repeat.
Short version:
*k1, p1; rep from * to the end of round.

Long version:
k1, p1, k1, p1, k1, p1.....

( ): used to include different sizes within the parentheses, separated by commas, for example s (m, l, xl). Before beginning your pattern, highlight all the instructions for the size you are following.

Reading charts

Many of the patterns use charts instead of written stitch patterns.
The charts are pictorial representation of the stitch patterns, color patterns, or shaping patterns.
   Reading charts in loom knitting differs from reading a chart when needle knitting. In needle knitting, the knitting is turned after every row, exposing the wrong and right side of the fabric on alternate rows. In loom knitting, the right side of the fabric is always to the front, so we follow the pictorial chart as it appears.

- Charts are visual and pictorial representations of the stitch pattern. A chart allows you to see the entire stitch pattern.
- Charts are numbered on both sides, even numbers on the right side, odd on the left.
- Start reading the chart from the bottom.
- Each square represents a stitch.
- Each horizontal row of squares represents a row.
- Stitch pattern charts use symbols to represent stitches such as knit, purl, twists, yarn overs, and any other stitch manipulation needed.
- Thick black lines represent the end of a pattern repeat. The stitches after the black line are edge, or selvedge, stitches.
- Charts for color knitting differ from stitch pattern charts. In color pattern charts each different color square represents the color needed for that particular stitch.
- For circular knitting, read the chart from bottom up from right to left.
- For flat knitting, read the chart from bottom up from right to left on odd rows, and from left to right on even rows.
- Remember that the right side of the knitted fabric is always facing the outside. Work the stitches as they appear on the chart.

Legend:

☐ **knit**
knit stitch

▣ **purl**
purl stitch

Chart reads:
For flat knitting:
Row 1: k2, p2
Row 2: p2, k2
Row 3: p2, k2
Row 4: k2, p2
For circular knitting:
Round 1: k2, p2
Round 2: k2, p2
Round 3: p2, k2
Round 4: p2, k2

A complete list of chart symbols and abbreviations used in this book is provided on page 140 (we are using needle knitting standard abbreviations and symbols whenever possible).

Materials and tools

Yarn

The choice is endless in today's yarn market, but there is plenty to take into consideration. When choosing your sock yarn, keep in mind these three concepts.

Climate: If the wearer lives in a warm climate, perhaps cotton will be more suitable. For colder climates a wool or wool blend will ensure toasty toes.

Lifestyle: Are the socks meant for a recipient who does a lot of outdoor activities? Perhaps a breathable but warm fiber such as wool would be best suited to them.

Yarn care: Many machine-washable yarns are now available, but the socks will last longer if they are hand washed and air dried. For tips on keeping your socks looking their best, and how to decode care symbols, see page 33.

Fiber content

In the market, you can find yarns made from all sorts of natural and synthetic fibers. The most commonly used for socks are wools, wool blends, and cottons.

Wool: Warm. Elastic. Durable. Some machine-washable. Good for: Comfort, warmth. Bad for: Allergies.

Cotton: Absorbs moisture quickly and dries quickly. Inelastic. Non-allergic. Machine-washable. Good for: Kids socks. Bad for: Elasticity.

Synthetics: Elastic and without elastic. Some non-allergic. Machine-washable. Non-absorbent. Good for: Washing. Bad for: Absorbency, comfort.

Yarn weight

Socks can be made from virtually any yarn in the market. Decide what shoes you are going to wear with the socks you are making. For thick socks, try worsted weight yarn. A thinner yarn such as sports weight or fingering weight will be better suited under shoes. For cozy bed socks, use bulky or chunky weight yarns.

Yarn Weight Symbol	1 SUPER FINE	2 FINE	3 LIGHT	4 MEDIUM	5 BULKY	6 SUPER BULKY
Types of Yarn	Sock, Fingering, Baby	Sports, Baby	DK Light, Worsted	Worsted, Aran	Chunky	Bulky
Knit Gauge in stockinette stitch per inch	7–8	5–6	4–5	3–4	2–3	1.5–2

How much yarn?

Obtaining the correct amount of yarn is crucial, especially if you are working with hand-painted sock yarn. You want to obtain all the yarn you are going to need in one trip to ensure that you buy the same dye lot. Take a look at the table below and the suggested yardage. Make a copy and keep it in your knitting bag to have handy when you go shopping.

> **TIP**
>
> Working cotton socks with an elastic thread can give more elasticity.

Approximate yardage (meters) needed for a pair of socks

Yarn weight	Child (small)	Youth	Woman	Man
Fingering	275 yd (252 m)	340 yd (311 m)	430 yd (393 m)	525 yd (480 m)
Sport	215 yd (197 m)	275 yd (252 m)	370 yd (339 m)	430 yd (393 m)
Worsted	200 yd (183 m)	250 yd (229 m)	340 yd (311 yd)	400 yd (366 m)
Bulky	185 yd (169 m)	215 yd (197 m)	310 yd (284 m)	370 yd (339 m)

Reinforcement yarn

Reinforcement yarn is used to reinforce the parts of the sock that get the most wear—heel and toes. You can find reinforcement yarn of every color in many yarn shops and online vendors. To use reinforcement yarn, simply work it along with the regular yarn when you are working on the heel and the toe areas.

Looms

Making socks on looms is easy, all you really need is to find a loom that makes the desired tube circumference.

Most of the patterns in this book were created using a knitting loom with an extra fine gauge or sett. Knitting looms that have pegs spaced at this measurement are perfect to create socks that are made with sock weight yarn, also known as fingering weight. Other socks in this book were made using a round loom along with chunky or super bulky weight yarn to create house socks or socks that can be worn with boots.

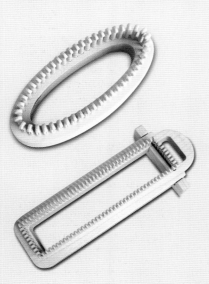

Looms with an extra fine gauge which have been used for the socks in this book include (from top to bottom), the 48 Peg EFG sock loom (Décor Accents) which is perfect for toe-up socks, and the Wonder Sock EFG loom (Décor Accents).

Useful tools

Knitting tool or pick
A knitting tool is generally made out of metal, with a wood or plastic handle. They come with different ends—some sharp to allow you to use them when knitting on very small pegs and with fingering weight yarns.

Scissors or yarn cutters
Many synthetic yarns and cottons are almost impossible to break so carrying small scissors in your knitting bag is always advisable.

Stitch gauge guide
A stitch guide allows you to determine exactly the number of stitches and rows per inch (or cm) in your work.

Row counter
A row counter is a little gadget that helps you keep track of the rows or rounds knitted.

Crochet hooks
Handy when picking up dropped stitches, these come in different sizes for different yarn weights.

Double pointed knitting needles
These will help the grafting process (see page 17). Keep two sets, one in size 8 (5 mm) and one in a size 1 (2.25 mm).

Tapestry needles
These are perfect to work with knitted fabric as the blunt tip reduces the problem of splitting the yarn. Use tapestry needles for weaving the yarn ends and when grafting. They also come in handy during seaming for some of the projects.

Stitch markers
Usually used in needle knitting, these are small rings that can be used to mark the pegs where special stitches will be made on the knitted item. Since they are small rings, they fit perfectly over the loom pegs and they can sit at the base of the loom.

Measuring tape and ruler
Discard any measuring tape at the first sign of distortion. A small plastic ruler is also advisable to have on hand.

Calculator
This is very handy when calculating gauge or even adding a few pegs to the count in the pattern.

Using the loom

Clockwise method

START

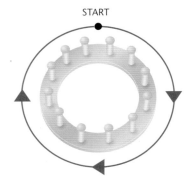

Counterclockwise method

START

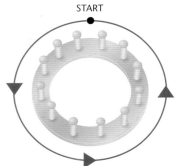

In loom knitting there are two schools of thought—the clockwise and counterclockwise methods.

In the clockwise method, you will work around your knitting loom in a clockwise direction. Begin knitting on the left side of the starting peg.

In the counterclockwise school of thought, you will find yourself working around the knitting loom in a counterclockwise direction. You will begin knitting on the peg to the right of your starting peg.

Both of the methods achieve the same goal. Choose the one that feels most comfortable to you, as the knitting still looks the same.

Note: when reading patterns, find out in which direction the pattern is worked. If you read the pattern in the wrong direction, you will end up with a mirror image of the design.

The designs in this book are worked in a **clockwise** direction around the knitting loom.

Loom anatomy

There are some basic parts to the loom that you will become increasingly familiar with. This is a circular loom, but the elements are the same whether it is rake, board, or round.

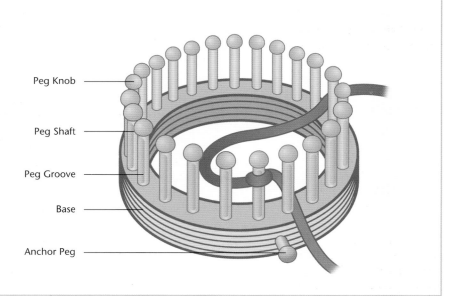

Peg Knob

Peg Shaft

Peg Groove

Base

Anchor Peg

Casting on

The foundation row for our loom knits is called the cast-on row, abbreviated as CO. Every cast-on method starts with a slip knot.

Slip knot

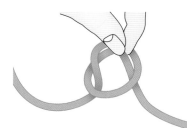

1 Leaving a 5-inch (12.5-cm) beginning tail, form a circle with the working yarn. Fold the circle over the working yarn that is coming from the skein.

2 Reach through the circle, and grab the yarn coming from the skein.

3 Pull the working yarn through the circle, while also pulling gently on the short end of the yarn tail end, thus tightening the noose on the knot.

The e-wrap cast-on (CO)

This cast on is called the e-wrap because if you look at it from an aerial view it resembles a cursive "e." It is the easiest method to learn. Use the e-wrap cast-on method when the first row needs to be picked up for a brim or seam, or when the cast-on row needs to be extremely flexible.

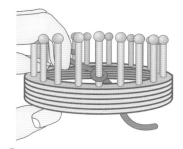

1 Place a stitch marker on any of the pegs on the knitting loom. The peg with the stitch marker will be your starting peg. Make a slip knot, and place it on the peg with the stitch marker.

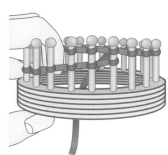

3 Wrap each peg a second time in the same method. Each peg should have two loops on it. Hold the working yarn in place so the wraps do not unravel.

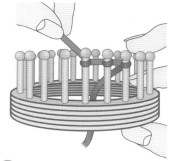

2 Holding the loom in front of you with the working yarn in your left hand, work around the knitting loom in a clockwise direction thus: * Pull the working yarn toward the inside of the loom, wrap around the peg directly to the left, in a counterclockwise direction around the peg. * Repeat from * to * with each of the pegs. Continue wrapping each peg in a counterclockwise direction, until you complete one round (each peg should have one loop). Notice how the yarn crosses over itself on the inside of the knitting loom.

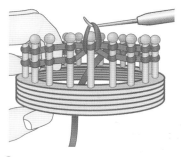

4 With the knitting tool, insert the tip of the tool into the bottommost loop on the last peg wrapped. Lift the loop up and off the peg and allow the loop to fall toward the inside of the knitting loom. The process of lifting the loops off the pegs is known as knitting over, abbreviated as ko. Go to the peg directly to the left and repeat step 4, knitting over. Repeat all around the loom until each peg has only one wrap. Steps 1–4 constitute the casting on set-up. Ready, set, go!

Casting on (continued)

Long tail cast-on

This is known as the long tail cast-on because you use the tail of the yarn and the working yarn to create the cast on. This is the same term used in needle knitting. It creates a flexible cast-on.

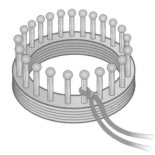

1 Make a slip knot, leaving a tail that is about four times as long as the width of your project. Place the slip knot on a peg. The slip knot will become your first stitch.

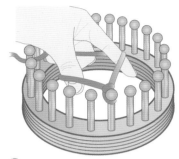

2 Position your left hand palm down: wrap the working yarn (the one coming from the skein) around your index finger and the tail over your thumb. Hold both yarn ends with the remaining three fingers.

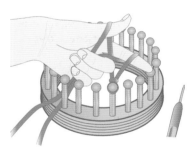

3 Flip your hand toward the left until your palm faces up. The hand is now in a slingshot position.

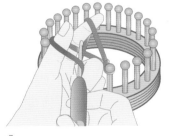

4 Guide the crochet hook by the palm side of the thumb under the yarn strand, then guide it over to the yarn strand on the index finger, hook the yarn strand on the index finger, and guide it down through the loop on your thumb.

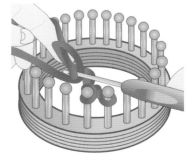

5 Place the loop on the adjacent empty peg. Remove your thumb from its loop and gently tug on the yarn tail to tighten the new stitch that you created. Repeat steps 3–5 until you have the number of stitches called for in the pattern.

No crochet hook?

There is a method of using long tail cast-on without a crochet hook but it is slightly more complicated.

1 With the slip knot on your first peg, grab the tail yarn and e-wrap the peg to the left. The peg now has two loops, knit over so only one loop remains.

2 Grab yarn coming from the skein and e-wrap the next empty peg.

3 Grab the tail yarn and place it above the e-wrap done in step 2. Lift the bottom loop over and off the peg (the peg should remain wrapped with the tail).

4 Repeat steps 2 and 3 with the remaining pegs.

TIPS

● You may find it more comfortable to place the loom on your lap or table to work on the cast-on.

● When making your slip knot, it is better to overestimate and make the tail too long rather than too short.

Basic stitches

The two basic stitches are the knit, or plain, and purl stitches. With these two stitches under your belt you will be able to create numerous stitch patterns for your loom knits.

Knit stitch (k)

The knit stitch is the cornerstone of any loom-knitted item. Known also as the plain stitch, the knit stitch resembles the knit stitch created on knitting needles. It looks like a small V. Variations on the knit stitch are known as the flat stitch and the u-stitch.

   Preparation: The knitting loom must have at least one stitch on each peg (a cast-on row).

KNIT STITCH BASICS

Knit stitch: Tall height and wider stitch
U-stitch: Medium height and medium width
Flat stitch: Short height and narrower width

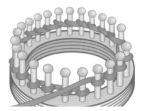 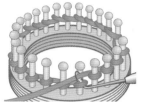 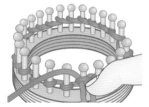 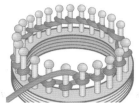

1 Lay the working yarn in front and above the stitch on the peg.

2 Insert the knitting tool through the stitch on the peg from bottom up. You will hook the working yarn where red ring indicates.

3 Hook the working yarn with the knitting tool, making a loop. Grab the loop with your fingers.

4 Take the original loop off the peg and replace with the new. Tighten the working yarn. Repeat steps 1–4 to complete a row.

Flat stitch (fs)

This variation looks exactly like the knit stitch, except it is a shorter and tighter stitch.

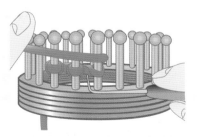 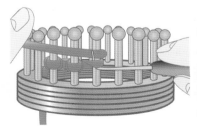 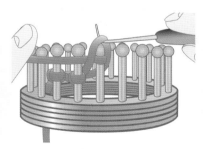

1 Take working yarn to the front of the peg and place it above the loop on the peg. Do not place any tension on it, simply rest it above.

2 Insert tool through the loop.

3 Lift the loop off the peg.

Basic stitches (continued)

U-stitch (u-st)

This variation also looks exactly like the knit stitch, except it is a shorter and tighter stitch. However, it is a little bigger, and not as tight as the flat stitch.

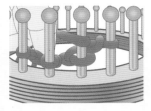 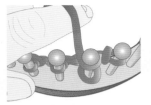 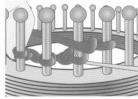 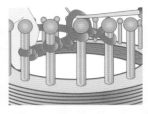

1 Take working yarn to the front of the peg and place it above the loop on the peg.

2 Wrap the working yarn around the peg, as if hugging the peg with the yarn.

3 Insert the knitting tool through the loop on the peg.

4 Lift the loop off the peg.

Purl stitch (p)

The purl stitch is the reverse of a knit stitch and shows as a small horizontal bump on the front.

   Preparation: The knitting loom must have at least one stitch on each peg (a cast-on row).

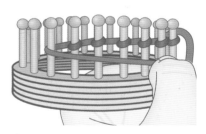 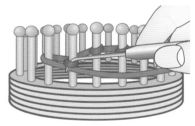 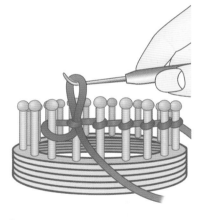

1 Lay the working yarn in front of and below the stitch on the peg.

2 Insert the knitting tool from top to bottom through the stitch on the peg and scoop up the working yarn with the knitting tool.

3 Pull the working yarn through the stitch on the peg to form a loop. Hold the new loop with your fingers.

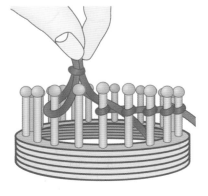

4 Take the old loop off the peg and place the new loop on the peg. Tug gently on the working yarn to tighten the stitch. Repeat steps 1–4 to complete a purl row.

Bringing up the cast-on row

We use this technique to create a picot edge when loom knitting socks.

Preparation: Work as many rows as indicated in pattern.

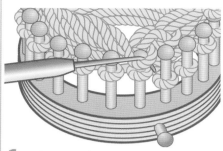

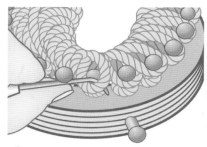

1 Reach inside the knitting loom, and find the beginning yarn tail end. Align the beginning yarn tail end with the first peg on the knitting loom. Next to the beginning tail end, locate the very first cast-on stitch. Place the stitch on the corresponding peg. Repeat this step with the remaining stitches. Each peg should have two loops on it.

2 Knit over by lifting the bottom loop off the peg. After all the stitches have been knitted over, the loom should only have one loop on each peg.

Binding off

Although it is the last step in creating the projects, binding off holds as much importance as any other part of the knitted item and has an impact on how the final socks will look.

Basic bind-off
This creates a firm, crochet-like edge. It can be used at the end of a project to cast off all the stitches, as well as when you have to bind off only a certain amount of stitches to make an opening.

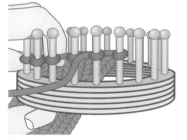

1 Knit two stitches (pegs 1 and 2).

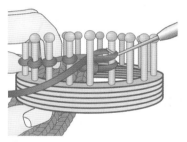

2 Move the loop from the second peg over to the first peg. Knit over.

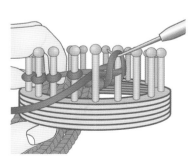

3 Move the loop on the first peg over to the peg just emptied.

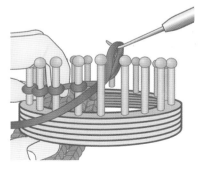

4 Knit the next peg. Repeat steps 2–4 until you have bound off the required number of stitches. A stitch will remain on the last peg. Cut the yarn leaving a long tail. E-wrap the peg, knit over, and pull the tail end through the stitch.

Binding off (continued)

Yarn over bind-off

The yarn over bind-off provides a stretchy border, perfect for items that need flexible openings. So it's a recommended bind-off for toe-up socks, as it provides a good flexible opening for the cuff.

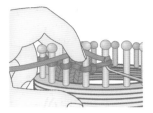

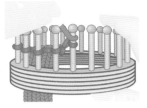

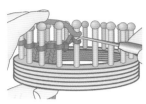

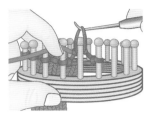

1 Knit the first stitch (peg 1).

2 Wrap the peg in a clockwise direction.

3 Knit over and knit the next stitch (peg 2).

4 Move the loop from the second peg to the first. Knit over. Repeat steps 2–4 until one stitch remains. Cut the yarn leaving a tail. E-wrap the peg, knit over, and pull the tail end through.

Gather bind-off

The gather removal method allows you to finish a tube into a gathered end, perfect for finishing socks. Knit the tube until you have reached the desired length.

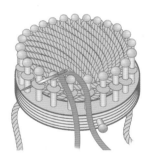

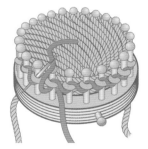

1 Cut the working yarn coming from the project, leaving a 5-inch (12.5-cm) tail. Or, if necessary, cut another piece of yarn that is at least twice the circumference of the knitting loom. Thread the yarn through a tapestry needle.

2 Go to the first peg, and pass the needle and yarn through the loop on the peg, leaving a 5-inch (12.5-cm) tail. Go to the second peg and pass the needle and yarn through the loop on the peg. Continue around the loom until you reach the last peg. Pass the needle and thread through the first stitch once more.

3 Remove the loops off the pegs. Gently pull on the beginning and end tails of the gathering yarn. Continue pulling on the tail ends until the top of the item is closed. Use the tapestry needle to sew the hole closed.

4 Grab the yarn tail end coming from the knitting of the project. Tie the three strands (the two ends from the gathering yarn and the one from the knitting of the project) together. Make a square knot and weave in the ends.

Grafting

Also known as the kitchener stitch, grafting allows us to join two panels of knitted fabric invisibly. The process is simple, although at first it may seem daunting, but take it step by step and you will be on your way to invisible seams. In the case of our socks, the toe area is grafted to the instep of the sock.

When you are preparing for grafting, you need to mount the stitches correctly on the needle. Correct position ensures proper grafting. Imagine the following: the knit stitch has a head and two arms: a right and a left arm. While holding the needle on the left hand, the stitches should sit on the needle with the right hand toward the front of the work.

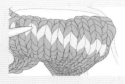

1 The stitches should look like this illustration.

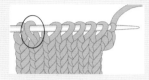

2 Not like this (note how the left leg toward the front of the needle is facing left).

Preparation

1 Cut working yarn coming from the sock, leaving a 3-yard (3-m) tail.
2 Transfer half of the stitches from the loom onto one double-pointed needle (in our example, loops from pegs 1 through 12).
3 Transfer the remaining half of the stitches to a second double-pointed needle (in our example, loops from pegs 13 through 24).
4 Thread a tapestry needle with the 3-yard (3-m) tail.

Working

For illustration purposes, a contrasting color yarn is used for the grafting row in our illustrations.

1 Hold knitting needles parallel to each other, wrong sides of the knitting together. Insert the tip of the tapestry needle through the first stitch on the front needle as if you were going to purl.

2 Insert yarn through the first stitch on the back needle as if to knit, pull the yarn through but leave stitch on the knitting needle.

3 Insert the tip of the tapestry needle through the first stitch on the front needle as if you were going to knit, pull the yarn through the stitch, and slide that same stitch off the needle.

4 Insert the yarn needle through the next stitch on the front needle as if to purl, pull the yarn through, and leave the stitch on the needle.

5 Bring the yarn to the side of the fabric (not over the needles) and insert the tapestry needle through the first stitch on the back needle as if to purl, bring the yarn through and slide the stitch off the needle.

6 Insert the tapestry needle through the next stitch on the back needle as if to knit, pull the yarn through and leave the stitch on the needle.

7 Repeat steps 3–6 across the row of stitches until only one stitch remains. Insert the tapestry needle through that last stitch and weave in ends.

TIP

If there are any uneven stitches, use the tapestry needle to gently tug on the little legs of the adjacent stitch until the stitches look even throughout the row.

Color and design

It is easy to jazz up a simple pattern by doing color changes along the way. Take a chance and create a wild project with some odd skeins left from other projects.

Stripes

Creating stripes is the easiest method to spice up a project. Knitting with stripes allows you to use as many colors as you wish without having to carry more than one color at a time within the row.

Designing with stripes is easy—gather all your odd skeins and sit down and loom knit a unique item. You could try anything from wide stripes, narrow stripes, to mixing wild colors and textured yarns.

Your one-of-a-kind creation will have one main color (MC) with one (or more) contrasting colors (CC). When more than one contrasting color is used, the colors are designated by letters, such as A, B, C, D, and so on.

Horizontal stripes

Knit a few rows with your main color. When it's time to change to a new color, join the new yarn at the beginning of a row (see page 32).

After you have your desired colors set up, you can carry the color along the edge of the item if knitting thin stripes. If you are knitting wider stripes, cut the yarn at the end of a row, and join yarns at the beginning of a row.

Vertical stripes

Creating thin vertical stripes is simple, and weaving the yarns at the back of the work is not required. The unused yarn can be carried behind the work. You will need yarn in two colors: a main color (MC) and a contrasting color (CC).

1 Pick up the MC and knit the stitches you desire in the main color, skip the ones you desire in contrasting color.
2 Go back to the beginning of the row, pick up the CC and knit all the pegs skipped in step 1. Repeat steps 1–2 throughout.

TIP

Jogless stripes

First round with contrasting color: work normally.
Second round with CC: **skip the first stitch** with yarn to the back of the stitch, work the rest of the stitches as indicated on the pattern.
Consecutive rounds with CC: work normally.
Repeat above steps when creating more stripes.

There is an amazing array of colors on the market—sometimes they can speak for themselves in projects such as the Guppy socks (page 46).

Loom knitting Fair Isle

The art of Fair Isle loom knitting is a technique of multicolored knitting, where a row is worked with only two colors in small repeating sections of patterns.

Traditional Fair Isle knitting is worked completely in stockinette stitch and the items are usually circular. The circular nature of the item helps to hide the floats created by the color changes within the row. When carrying the unused color, it is recommended not to carry it over more than 5–7 stitches, or 1–1.5 inches (2.5–4 cm).

Fair Isle patterns are usually depicted in chart form and share some characteristics with regular knitting charts. Each square represents a stitch. The squares will either be colored in or will have a color symbol and key. For circular knitting, you read the chart starting at the bottom, right side. Continue reading the next rounds starting at the right side.

Although it may seem complicated, the process of painting with your yarn is quite simple. There are two methods that you can use.

Method 1: This keeps your yarns separated and untangled. You pick up the main color at the beginning of a row, knit the required stitches then drop it at the end of the row. Pick up the contrasting color and knit all the required stitches with that color, then drop it.

Method 2: You carry both yarns with you in your dominant hand as you work the stitch pattern. When the pattern calls for the CC, drop the MC color and bring the CC above the MC working yarn, knit as required. When the pattern calls for the MC, drop the CC, reach below for the MC color. Every time you change yarns, drop the new one above then reach below for the other.

To weave the yarns around each other: knit a few stitches with the MC color, drop it and pick up the CC, wrap the CC around the MC, drop the CC, pick up the MC and keep on knitting. Take both colors to the back of the work, and twist them together.

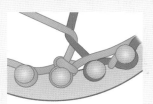

Weave the two colors around each other at the back of the work to prevent holes showing.

Cables

A cable is a design feature that creates a rope-like twist in the knitting. The rope-like twist is created by placing a few stitches on hold on a cable needle, so that the stitches may be worked out of their usual order. Although cables may seem a bit intimidating at first, with practice you will notice that they are quite simple.

Cables work best when worked with yarns that have some inherent elasticity—for instance yarns with wool content. Use a cable needle or a double-pointed needle to hold your stitches while you cross them.

When creating a cable, the stitches on the right side of the loom (when the loom is facing you) are held on the cable needle (without being worked) while you work on the stitches to the left. Depending on the type of lean you want on your cable, you will hold the cable needle either toward the center of the loom or toward the front of the loom.

If the cable needle is held in front of the work, the cable will twist to the left. This is the left cross (LC), also known as front cross (FC).

If the cable needle is held to the center of the loom (back of work) the cable will have a right twist. This is the right cross (RC), also known as the back cross (BC).

Left cross (LC)—2 stitches

1 Take working yarn behind peg 1 (you are skipping peg 1).

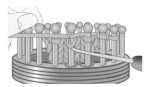

2 Knit peg 2 and place stitch on cable needle and hold it to the center of the loom.

3 Move stitch from peg 1 to peg 2 (leaving peg 1 empty).

4 Place stitch from cable needle on peg 1.

5 Knit peg 2.

> ### Purl cables with 2 stitches
>
> Achieving left cross purl (LCP) and right cross purl (RCP) cables is easy.
> **LCP**: Follow the left cross (LC) instructions, except in step 2, purl instead of knit peg 2.
> **RCP**: Follow the right cross (RC) instructions, except in step 5, purl instead of knit peg 2.

Right cross (RC)—2 stitches

1 Place stitch from peg 1 on cable needle and hold to the center of the knitting loom.

2 Take working yarn in front of peg 2 and knit peg 2.

3 Move stitch from peg 2 to peg 1.

4 Place stitch from cable needle on peg 2.

5 Knit peg 2.

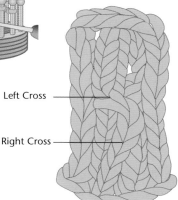

Left Cross

Right Cross

Left cross (LC)—3 stitches

1 Take working yarn behind pegs 1 and 2 (you are skipping pegs 1 and 2).

2 Knit peg 3. Place stitch from peg 3 onto cable needle.

3 Knit peg 1 and peg 2. Move them over to pegs 2 and 3 as follows: Stitch from peg 2 to peg 3, stitch from peg 1 to peg 2.

4 Place stitch from cable needle onto peg 1.

Right cross (RC)—3 stitches

1 Place stitch from peg 1 to cable needle and hold to center of knitting loom.

4 Place the stitch from cable needle on peg 3. Knit peg 3.

Right cross (RC)—4 stitches

1 Take working yarn behind pegs 1 and 2 (you are skipping pegs 1 and 2).

2 Knit peg 3 and 4. Place loops from pegs 3 and 4 on cable needle.

3 Knit pegs 1 and 2. Move them over as follows: Stitch from peg 2 to peg 4; stitch from peg 1 to peg 3.

4 Take the stitches off the cable needle and place them on pegs 1 and 2.

5 Go to each of the stitches on pegs 1–4 and gently pull out any yarn slack so it tightens the cable.

Left cross (LC)—4 stitches

1 Remove sts from pegs 1 and 2 and place them on cable needle.

2 Knit peg 3 and 4. Transfer stitches to pegs as follows: Stitch from peg 3 to peg 1; stitch from peg 4 to peg 2.

3 Transfer the sts from cable needle to emptied pegs 3 and 4. Knit these 2 sts.

4 Go to each of the loops on pegs 1–4 and gently pull out any yarn slack so it tightens the cable.

2 Knit peg 2 and peg 3.

3 Move the stitches from pegs 2 and 3 to pegs 1 and 2.

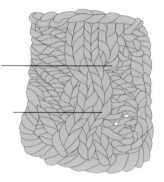

Left Cross

Right Cross

> **Purl cables with 3 stitches**
> To achieve left cross purl (LCP) and right cross purl (RCP) with 3 and 4 stitches, the crossing stitches are purled rather than knitted.
> **LCP**: At step 2, purl instead of knit peg 3.
> **RCP**: At step 4, purl instead of knit peg 3.

Lace

Lace can create wonderful effects on socks. Here are some techniques that will start you lacing in no time!

Slip, slip knit (ssk)

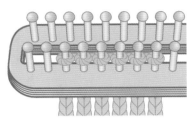

This creates a left slanting decrease. The process takes place over 2 pegs. Peg 1 is on the right and Peg 2 is on the left. Move stitch from second peg and place it on first peg and then treat both stitches on the second peg as one. You could also try a double decrease with 3 pegs instead of 2.

Knitting 2 together (k2tog)

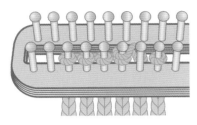

This creates a right slanting decrease, and takes place over 2 pegs. Peg 1 is on the right and peg 2 is on the left. Move stitch from first peg over to the second peg and then treat both stitches on the second peg as one.

Knitting 3 together (k3tog)

This is very similar to the k2tog but takes place over 3 pegs. Peg 1 is on the right, peg 2 is in the middle, peg 3 is on the left. Move the stitch from peg 2 over to peg 3. Move both stitches from peg 3 over to peg 2, move the stitch from peg 1 to peg 2. Peg 2 now has 3 loops on it. Move all three loops over to peg 1 and then treat 3 loops as one.

Beads

Including beads in your work can make an ordinary project extraordinary! Do not be afraid to add them to your projects, the process is simple and it provides beautiful results.

Preparation: Before you can begin working with beads, you need to pre-thread them onto the yarn.

1 Using a sewing needle and nylon thread, slide all the beads onto the thread.

2 Tie the end of the thread to the beginning of the yarn and slide all the beads down onto the yarn. Once all the beads are on the yarn, cut the nylon thread and you can begin working.

Placing the beads

1 Take working yarn to the front of the peg where you want the bead located.

2 Slide the bead down as closely as possible to the front of the peg.

3 Take the stitch off the peg and hold it.

4 With knitting tool, lift the bead from Step 2 and place it behind the peg.

5 Place the stitch back on the peg and take working yarn to the front of the loom.

6 Work the next peg as indicated in the pattern.

Measuring for gauge on socks

With all the basic information on board, you are ready to take on your first pattern. Before you move on to Sock 101, you must make a swatch to test your gauge. It can be time-consuming, but you definitely need to work up a swatch before you knit socks. Do not let them fool you—despite their small size, an average sock can have about 64 stitches per round and about 12 rows in an inch (2.5 cm). This translates into 768 stitches in one inch (2.5 cm) of work so, if you unravel half a sock, you can be wasting about 4,600 stitches. Trust me, it is easier to work up a swatch than to start over from the beginning.

A swatch needs to be worked in the round and in the stitch pattern for the sock. Work a tube swatch that is about 5 inches (12 cm) in length, adding a ribbing at the beginning and a ribbing at the end. Take the swatch off the loom with a basic bind-off (see page 15). Check the swatch for gauge. Check the gauge at three or four different places to ensure accuracy.

If you have more or fewer stitches and rows than the pattern calls for, your stitches are either too small or too big, so try a different yarn weight or a different version of the stitch (for example, swap knit stitch for u-stitch or flat stitch). The tube that you created during the swatch process can now be used for different purposes: cup cozy, wrist band, or even a sandal sock!

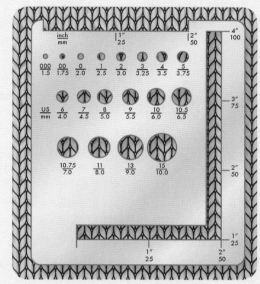

A stitch gauge allows you to determine exactly the number of stitches and rows per inch (or cm) in your work.

Keep your socks-in-progress in bags like these ones (right), from KnowKnits. They are light weight and have great snap closures that make them easy to attach to any regular bag. They come in different sizes to fit all your project needs.

YOU WILL NEED

Knitting loom

● Large gauge knitting loom with 24 pegs (small round Blue Knifty Knitter loom used in sample).

Yarn

● 250 yds (230 m) bulky weight yarn. (Sample uses GGH Aspen, 50% fine merino wool 50% microfiber, 126 yd [115 m] per 1¾ oz [50 g] in sand.)

5 BULKY

Tools

● 2 double pointed needles size 8 (5 mm)

● Tapestry needle

Gauge

● 6 sts and 8 rows to 2 inches

Top-down:
1. Cuff
2. Leg
3. Heel
4. Foot
5. Toe

Sock 101

Top-down method

As our introduction so far has been about the basic techniques, here everything is put together for a trial top-down sock, from the cast on to the grafting stage.

One of the most important aspects of a sock is the cast on. A non-flexible cast on can make for uncomfortable socks—while you may be able to get your foot in, once it is on your leg it can cut circulation. You want a flexible yet firm cast on that will hold the stitches nicely and hold up to the use that a sock gets.

In our sample sock, we are going to work a woman's medium size slipper sock using bulky weight yarn and our large gauge loom. The slipper is knitted at a large gauge of 3 stitches per inch (2.5 cm). The first step in the process is to cast on the stitches onto our loom. We will use the long tail cast on (see page 12).

Preparation

Place a peg marker on whichever peg you want and designate it as your first peg. If you are using a loom with an anchor peg, then your first peg will be the one to the left of this anchor peg.

1 Using the long tail cast on method, cast on 24 stitches in a clockwise direction around the loom (follow instructions on page 12).
2 Join to work in the round (see page 27 for options).

Cuff: We will work our cuff in a 2x2 ribbing. The ribbing provides a stretchy fabric that will ensure a snug fit on the recipient.

A 2x2 ribbing is worked by knitting 2 pegs (see page 13), then purling 2 pegs (see page 14). Repeat the process until the entire round has been completed.

Continue ribbing by repeating the knit 2, purl 2 process until the cuff measures 2 inches (5 cm).

Leg: The leg portion of our sock is worked completely in stockinette stitch. After you have completed the 2 inch (5 cm) ribbing, continue working in the knit stitch. Continue knitting each round until the leg measures 6 inches (15 cm) from the cast-on edge.

Heel: The magic occurs in this section. Our simple tube is turned into a sock by a few short-rows.

The heel is worked on 50% of the sock stitches as a flat panel. Place a marker on the first peg and at the half-way point peg. In our practice sock, you will place a marker on the first peg and a marker on peg 12.

The anatomy of the sock

Socks can be knitted either toe-up, or top-down. In top-down socks, the sock is knitted in one single piece: It starts in the round, then it is knitted flat for the heel, then it is knitted in the round again for the foot, and finally the toe is knitted flat, and grafted.

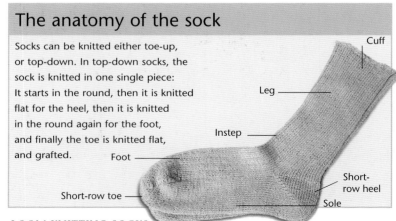

Cuff

Leg

Instep

Foot

Short-row toe

Short-row heel

Sole

How to wrap and turn

Shaping with short-rows has one pitfall that you must be aware of. It is necessary to wrap the stitch after the turning point to avoid a hole between the turning stitch and the next stitch. The wrap eliminates this almost completely.

1 Knit or purl to the desired turning stitch. Take the stitch off the next peg and hold it with your knitting tool.

2 Wrap the peg by taking the yarn toward the inside of the loom and wrapping around the peg. The working yarn will end up to the front of the knitting loom.

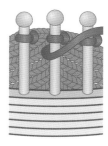

3 Place the stitch back on the peg. Take the working yarn and knit or purl back across the row.

Short-rows: A row that is not worked completely to the end, you work a portion of the row then turn and work in the other direction.

Short-row method

We will work on these 12 stitches using short-rows (rows that are only partially knitted) to create an area that has more fabric, which will accommodate the heel. The loom in the example has a stitch marker on the first peg and a stitch marker on the last heel peg (peg 12 for our example).

1 **Row 1**: Knit across all the stitches to one stitch before last, wrap the last peg (peg 12). The last peg is now wrapped and it remains unworked (not knitted). Turn knitting direction (toward peg 1).

2 **Row 2**: Knit across row to one stitch before last, wrap the peg. The last stitch is now wrapped, and it remains unworked. Turn knitting direction.

3 **Row 3**: Knit across the row to the peg before the last wrapped peg, wrap the peg. The last stitch is now wrapped, and it remains unworked. Turn knitting direction.

4 **Row 4**: Knit across to the peg before the last peg wrapped, wrap the peg. The last peg is now wrapped, and it remains unworked. Turn knitting direction.

5 Repeat rows 3 and 4 until 4 stitches remain unwrapped (you will have 4 wrapped stitches on the right, 4 unwrapped in the center, 4 wrapped on the left). End ready for a clockwise row (right to left).

A pair of top-down socks during the short-row process.

Avoiding holes on the last short-row

Many loom knitters have experienced this problem—they have worked a perfect heel only to end up with two big holes at each side of the last reverse short-row. To avoid these pesky holes, simply pick up the stitch from the row below and place it back on the peg. When you reach that peg, work both of the loops on the peg as one. Hole eliminated.

Reverse short-row shaping:

Note: Lift over the wraps first before working the stitch as this provides a cleaner wrap and turn.

Working the peg with the wraps

1 Place working yarn above the stitch on the peg, lift the wraps over and off the peg.
2 Knit the peg.

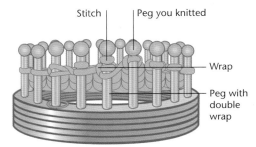

1 Row 1: Knit across to the first wrapped peg and knit it. Wrap the next peg, this peg now has two wraps and the stitch.

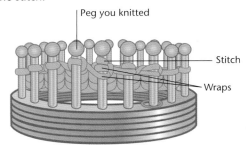

2 Row 2: Knit across to the first wrapped peg and knit it. Wrap the next peg, this peg now has two wraps and the stitch.

3 Repeat rows 1 and 2 until you have worked all the wrapped pegs. Be sure to lift both wraps over the stitch before knitting them together with the wrapped stitch. The heel's little pocket is done, bravo!

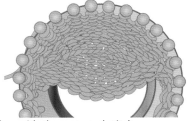

Foot: The foot is simple, just a tube and we already know how to work those. Start working in the round in stockinette stitch again (knitting all rounds). Work in the round until the foot measures 7 inches (18 cm) from the back of the heel.

Toe: The toe is another area where we need the extra fabric and we are going to create the extra fabric using short rows once again. Repeat the entire short-row shaping we did during the heel until you have worked all wrapped pegs.

Finish off the sock with the grafting technique on page 17.

Weaving in the tail ends

You have finished your first sock, and it is almost ready to be worn, but you still need to hide those unsightly tail ends from your yarn or your toes may get caught when you put your foot inside the sock. What to do? It is fairly simple, all you need is a large tapestry needle. Work carefully on the wrong side of the item and your stitches should be invisible.

Steps 1–2 should create a "Z" with the tail end. Cut the remainder of the yarn as close to the knitted item as possible. Repeat this process with each yarn tail end you have in your knitted item.

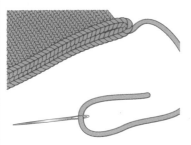

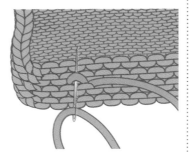

1 Locate the yarn tail end and thread it through the large eye of a tapestry needle.

2 Working on the wrong side of the item weave the yarn tail end by inserting the needle through the "bump" of each knit stitch. Go up and down one row for about 1 inch (2.5 cm) in each direction.

The top-down method produces projects like the Snaking socks (page 88).

Methods to join in the round

Simple join

Simply take the working yarn from the last peg over to the first peg and begin working your first round. There will be a small gap between the first and last peg, however you can close it with the tail end when you are done working on the sock.

Crossover join

In this case, the loop from the first peg exchanges places with the loop from the last peg. You will need to carefully remove the stitch from the first peg and hold it. Place the loop from the last peg over on the first peg. Place the loop you are holding on the last peg.

Tail-end join

When working the first round, pick up the working yarn and the tail coming from the slip knot. Treat both yarns as one and work the first three stitches with both yarns. These three stitches will have the double yarn— remember to pick up both when working on these three pegs on the next round.

YOU WILL NEED

Knitting loom

● Oval fine knitting loom with 36 pegs (Décor Accents 36 peg Oval child sock loom was used in this sample.)

Yarn

● 8–10 yd (7–9 m) of scrap yarn

● 185 yd (170 m) of any fingering weight yarn

Toe-up:
1. Toe
2. Foot
3. Heel
4. Leg

Toe-up method

A toe-up sock is one that is worked from the toe of the sock up to the cuff.

Toe-up sock construction has its appeal. Since you are working from the toe to the cuff, you can easily adapt the sock leg length to accommodate any yarn shortage.

One of the biggest appeals for most loom knitters is that no kitchener stitch is needed around the toe. Although there is no kitchener stitch, there is more knitting involved than in a top-down sock. However, although you may not need the kitchener stitch for this type of sock construction, it is advisable to learn this skill as it will come in handy in loom knitting other garments. This practice pattern makes a toddler size 8 sock.

The oval knitting loom makes it easier for the cast-on stitches to be placed back on the knitting loom. Although you can work toe-up method socks on round knitting looms, the oval shape makes it easier to pick up the stitches from the cast-on row and to stretch those stitches to the opposite side—as that opposite side is closer than if the shape was a circle.

Preparation:
Using the e-wrap cast on (see page 11), cast on with scrap yarn on half of the pegs—18 pegs for our sample. The working yarn should be ready for a clockwise row. Work 3 or 5 rows in knit stitch.

Toe and foot

1 Join main yarn, leaving a 5-inch (12.5-cm) tail for weaving in, and knit from peg 18 to peg 1.

2 Begin short-row shaping for the toe—the directions are the same as for the Top-down Sock (for instructions, see page 25) **However, repeat Rows 3 and 4 until 6 stitches remain unwrapped (you will have 6 wrapped stitches on the right, 6 unwrapped in the center, 6 wrapped on the left).** End ready for a clockwise row (right to left).

3 Begin reverse short-row shaping (for instructions, see page 26).

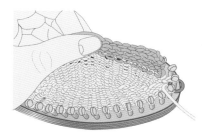

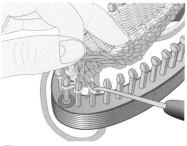

4 When the toe is completed, you will have a small panel knitted.

5 The next step—bringing the first row to the opposite side of the loom—is crucial. The scrap yarn you used to knit the first few rows will help in identifying the first row. With the aid of a knitting tool, bring the first row that was worked with the main yarn and place those stitches on the empty pegs at the opposite side of the loom.

Removing the scrap yarn

1 Turn sock inside out.
2 With scissors, carefully clip off the beginning tail of the scrap yarn.
3 Use the knitting tool to assist in unraveling the rows knitted with scrap yarn.

Turn sock right side out and admire your work!

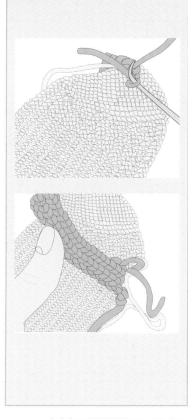

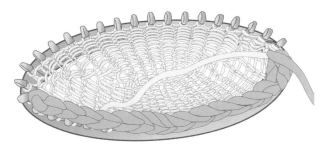

6 Once all the stitches (18 stitches in this example) have been placed on the empty pegs, the toe is complete.

Work in the round in stockinette stitch (knit every round) until foot measures 4 inches (10 cm) from the beginning of the toe.

Heel shaping

Repeat the short-row shaping instructions (see page 26) as previously worked for the toe.

Cuff

Work 2 rnds in stockinette stitch (knit every round).
Work 8 rnds in 2x2 Rib stitch (*k2, p2; rep from * to the end of rnd).
Bind off loosely with basic bind-off method (see page 15).

Designing your own socks

Short-row socks are loom knitted using the following percentage formula: 100%, 50%, 30%, 50%, 100%, and lastly 50%. What do all these numbers mean?

Follow the diagram to see the different measurements you need. You will need the leg length, foot length from heel to big toe, and the foot circumference around the ball of the foot.

Socks are usually worn snugly around the foot, and for this reason, socks are made with a negative ease. Usually a 10–15% negative ease. Remember the negative ease when choosing the loom for your socks.

The measurement obtained from the widest part of the foot, usually the ball of the foot, becomes the circumference of the sock—the 100%. The cuff and the leg portion of the socks are worked over 100% of the stitches.

The heel stitches are worked over 50% of the stitches as a flat panel, and short-rows are introduced at this point to create a cup to give the heel its form. The short-rows are worked in one direction, decreasing the 50% down to 30%. Then the flat panel is worked in the other direction, increasing back to 50% of the heel stitches. The same number of rows that were worked to go down to the 30% are worked to go back up to the 50% of heel stitches. The heel in a sense forms an hourglass shape.

The foot of the sock is worked over 100% of the stitches, just like the cuff and the leg of the sock. The toe is created the same way as the heel, with 50% of the stitches. The short-rows are worked in both decrease and increase directions to form the cup that will house the toes.

Using the formula

Using the formula above, you will soon be on your way to designing your own socks! You will calculate the number of stitches needed for the sock. First you need to measure the recipient's foot so you can work the socks to those measurements.

As an example, let's assume the circumference of the foot is 6½ inches (16.5 cm) and we are working at a gauge of 4 stitches per inch (2.5 cm), giving us a total of 26 stitches. However, we need to account for the negative ease. In our example we are going to assume a 10% negative ease. Based on these numbers, we will need a knitting loom with 24 pegs. 24 pegs becomes our 100%, and after this, we can easily calculate the rest of the numbers.

The heel is worked on 50% of the leg stitches (12 pegs) and we short-row until we have 30% of the stitches unworked (4 pegs), then we short-row again until we get back to 50% (12 pegs). Finally, the foot is worked on 100% of the stitches (24 pegs) and the toe is worked on 50% of the stitches (12 pegs), repeating the short-row shaping process.

Child's shoe size	Foot Circumference	Leg Length	Total Foot
4	5 in. (12.7 cm)	2 ½ in. (6.4 cm)	4 ¼ in. (10.8 cm)
5	5 ¼ in. (13.4 cm)	3 ¼ in. (8.3 cm)	4 ¾ in. (12 cm)
6	5 ½ in. (14 cm)	3 ¼ in. (8.3 cm)	5 in. (12.7 cm)
7	5 ¾ in. (14.6 cm)	3 ½ in. (8.9 cm)	5 ¼ in. (13.4 cm)
8	6 ¼ in. (15.9 cm)	3 ¾ in. (9.5 cm)	5 ½ in. (14 cm)
9	6 ¼ in. (15.9 cm)	4 ¼ in. (10.8 cm)	6 in. (15.2 cm)
10	6 ¾ in. (17.2 cm)	4 ½ in. (11.4 cm)	6 ¼ in. (15.9 cm)
11	6 ¾ in. (17.2 cm)	4 ¾ in. (12 cm)	6 ¾ in. (17.2 cm)
12	6 ¾ in. (17.2 cm)	5 in. (12.7 cm)	7 in. (17.8 cm)
13	7 in. (17.8 cm)	5 ¼ in. (13.4 cm)	7 ⅜ in. (18.7 cm)

Woman's shoe size	Foot Circumference	Leg Length	Total Foot
5	7 ½ in. (19 cm)	6 ⅛ in. (15.6 cm)	8 ¾ in. (22.2 cm)
5 ½	7 ⅝ in. (19.2 cm)	6 ¼ in. (15.9 cm)	8 ⅞ in. (22.5 cm)
6	7 ¾ in. (19.7 cm)	6 ¼ in. (15.9 cm)	9 in. (22.9 cm)
6 ½	7 ⅞ in. (20 cm)	6 ½ in. (16.5 cm)	9 ¼ in. (23.5 cm)
7	8 ⅛ in. (20.6 cm)	6 ¾ in. (17.2 cm)	9 ⅜ in. (23.8 cm)
7 ½	8 ¼ in. (21 cm)	6 ¾ in. (17.2 cm)	9 ½ in. (24.1 cm)
8	8 ⅜ in. (21.3 cm)	6 ⅞ in. (17.5 cm)	9 ¾ in. (24.8 cm)
8 ½	8 ½ in. (21.6 cm)	7 in. (17.8 cm)	9 ¾ in. (24.8 cm)
9	8 ¾ in. (22.2 cm)	7 ¼ in. (18.4 cm)	10 in. (25.4 cm)
9 ½	8 ¾ in. (22.2 cm)	7 ¼ in. (18.4 cm)	10 ¼ in. (26 cm)
10	9 in. (22.9 cm)	7 ⅜ in. (18.7 cm)	10 ¼ in. (26 cm)
10 ½	9 ⅛ in. (23.2 cm)	7 ⅝ in. (19.2 cm)	10 ½ in. (26.7 cm)
11	9 ¼ in. (23.5 cm)	7 ¾ in. (19.7 cm)	10 ¾ in. (27.3 cm)
11 ½	9 ⅜ in. (23.8 cm)	7 ⅞ in. (20 cm)	10 ¾ in. (27.3 cm)
12	9 ½ in. (24.1 cm)	7 ⅞ in. (20 cm)	11 in. (27.9 cm)

Man's shoe size	Foot Circumference	Leg Length	Total Foot
6	8 ¼ in. (21 cm)	6 ½ in. (16.5 cm)	9 ⅜ in. (23.8 cm)
6 ½	8 ⅜ in. (21.3 cm)	6 ¾ in. (17.2 cm)	9 ⅝ in. (24.5 cm)
7	8 ½ in. (21.6 cm)	6 ¾ in. (17.2 cm)	9 ¾ in. (24.8 cm)
7 ½	8 ¾ in. (22.2 cm)	6 ⅞ in. (17.5 cm)	9 ¾ in. (24.8 cm)
8	8 ¾ in. (22.2 cm)	7 in. (17.8 cm)	10 in. (25.4 cm)
8 ½	9 in. (22.9 cm)	7 ⅛ in. (18.1 cm)	10 ¼ in. (26 cm)
9	9 ⅛ in. (23.2 cm)	7 ¼ in. (18.4 cm)	10 ¼ in. (26 cm)
9 ½	9 ¼ in. (23.5 cm)	7 ⅜ in. (18.7 cm)	10 ⅝ in. (27 cm)
10	9 ⅜ in. (23.8 cm)	7 ½ in. (19 cm)	10 ¾ in. (27.3 cm)
10 ½	9 ½ in. (24.1 cm)	7 ⅝ in. (19.2 cm)	10 ⅞ in. (27.6 cm)
11	9 ¾ in. (24.8 cm)	7 ¾ in. (19.7 cm)	11 in. (27.9 cm)
11 ½	9 ¾ in. (24.8 cm)	7 ¾ in. (19.7 cm)	11 ⅛ in. (28.3 cm)
12	10 in. (25.4 cm)	7 ⅞ in. (20 cm)	11 ¼ in. (28.6 cm)
12 ½	10 ⅛ in. (25.7 cm)	8 ⅛ in. (20.6 cm)	11 ½ in. (29.2 cm)
13	10 ¼ in. (26 cm)	8 ¼ in. (21 cm)	11 ⅝ in. (29.5 cm)
13 ½	10 ⅜ in. (26.4 cm)	8 ¼ in. (21 cm)	11 ¾ in. (29.9 cm)
14	10 ⅝ in. (27 cm)	8 ⅜ in. (21.3 cm)	12 in. (30.5 cm)
14 ½	10 ¾ in. (27.3 cm)	8 ½ in. (21.6 cm)	12 ⅛ in. (30.8 cm)

Adapting your heel

Use the following table when designing your own socks or when adapting some of the patterns in the book to a different size.

Find the loom peg count of the knitting loom you would like to use, and use the grid to see the number of pegs used for the heel, and the number that should remain unwrapped when working your short-rows. Remember, for a wider heel, leave more stitches unwrapped, and for a narrower heel, leave less stitches unwrapped.

Knitting loom peg count	Pegs used for the heel	Un-wrapped pegs
96	48	16
92	46	16
88	44	16
84	42	14
80	40	14
76	38	14
72	36	14
68	34	12
64	32	12
60	30	10
56	28	8
52	26	8
48	24	8
44	22	6
40	20	6
36	18	6
32	16	4
28	14	4
24	12	4

Fixing mistakes

So you have been happily knitting, then you look down, and horror, you see a stitch dangling all by itself. What do you do? If it is one or two stitches, we can save the day.

On stockinette side fabric

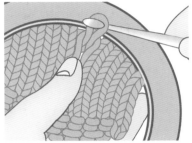

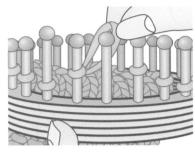

1 Insert the crochet hook from front to back through the stitch dropped.

2 Hook the first "ladder" or horizontal bar behind the stitch and pull it through the stitch to the front of the work.

3 Continue picking up the unraveled stitches by following step 2. When all stitches have been picked up, place the last stitch back on the peg.

On purl side fabric

1 Insert crochet hook through the back side of the fabric (inside the circle of the loom, or the wrong side of the fabric). Hook the dropped stitch.

2 Hook the unraveled strand behind the stitch and pull it through the stitch to the back of the fabric.

3 Continue picking up the unraveled stitches by following step 2. When all stitches have been picked up, place the last stitch back on the peg.

Joining yarns

When you least expect it, it happens—the yarn suddenly comes to an end, or worse, breaks. It is time to attach a new yarn to the project.

At the edge: Join the new yarn at the beginning of a row. If possible join the yarn on an edge that will be within a seam.

Method 1: Leave a tail of about 5–6 inches (12–15 cm) in length on the old skein and another tail the same length on the new skein. Hold the two yarns together and knit the first three stitches. Drop the old skein and continue knitting with the newly joined yarn.

Method 2: Leave a tail of about 5–6 inches (12–15 cm) in length on the old skein and another tail the same length on the new skein. Tie a temporary knot with the two ends as close to the project as possible. Pick up the newly joined yarn and continue knitting. When project is complete, go back and undo the knot, weave in the ends in the opposite direction to close the gap formed by the change of yarns.

Stuck in the middle: Occasionally you will need to join yarn in the middle of a row. Use method 2 above and tie a knot close to the project, making sure to leave a tail of about 5–6 inches (12–15 cm) on both ends. Continue knitting with the new yarn. Make sure to undo the knot before weaving in the ends.

Fixing stitches

If you accidentally knitted the wrong stitch on the row below, you have two options.

Option 1: Work back the row, one stitch at a time, until you reach the stitch where the mistake is located. Fix the stitch and continue knitting.

Option 2: Drop the stitch on that column of stitches and fix the mistake.

If the problem is located a few rows back, it is best to unravel the knitting and undo the entire row with the mistake.

1 Use a piece of waste yarn or a circular needle to hold your stitches to act as a lifeline one row below the problem row.

2 Take the stitches off the pegs and unravel all the stitches until you reach the row with the lifeline that is your stitch holder.

3 Place the stitches back on the pegs. Make sure to position the stitches on the loom the correct way.

Washing your knits

Hand washing is the best washing technique for all your knitted items. Even those items that were knitted with machine-washable yarns can have their life extended by practicing good washing habits.

- Use pure soap flakes or special wool soap. Wash and rinse your item gently in warm water. Maintain an even water temperature; changing water temperature can shock your wool items and accidentally felt them. Before washing, test for colorfastness. If the yarn bleeds, wash the item in cold water. If the yarn is colorfast, wash with warm water.

- Fill a basin or sink with water, add the soap flakes or wool soap, and using your hands, gently wash the knitted item. Avoid rubbing, unless you want the yarn to mat and felt together.

- To rinse, empty the basin and fill with clean warm water, immerse your knitted item and gently squeeze out all the soapsuds. Repeat until all the suds are gone and the water is soap free, changing the water as often as necessary. Pat as much of the water out as you can using the palms of your hands. Do not wring your item as this may cause wrinkles and distort the yarn. Place the knitted item between two towels and squeeze as much of the water out as you can.

- To dry your item, lay it flat away from direct sunlight. Block again, if necessary, to correct measurements.

Care symbols

Sock yarn label bands include a series of care symbols for the yarn. Following those instructions will ensure the best care for your loom-knitted socks. Although there can be variations, these symbols are the most well-known internationally.

 Not machine washable

 Hand wash

 Hand wash at indicated temperature

 Machine dry

 Do not machine dry

 Lay flat to dry

 No chlorine

 Chlorine

PART I
Simple socks

Single rib socks

Single rib socks are classic! The pattern is easily adaptable as it has a multiple of 2. Make a pair for everyone in the family.

LEVEL 1

MATERIALS

Knitting loom

64 peg extra fine gauge knitting loom. (WonderSock loom was used in this sample.)

Yarn

400–440 yd (365–402 m) of sock weight yarn. (Sample uses Scout's Swag, 100% superwash merino, 370–400yd [338–365 m] per 3½ oz [100 g] in Stocker Pond.)

1 SUPER FINE

Tools

Knitting tool
Tapestry needle
2 double pointed needles in size 1 (US)

Gauge

18 sts and 24 rows to 2 in. (5 cm) in St st (knit all rows)

Size

Shown in 9 in. (23 cm) foot circumference.

Adapt

Can be adapted to any other (smaller or larger) loom with a peg multiple of 2.

Stitch pattern:
Single rib stitch

Rnd 1: *k1, p1; rep from * to the end of rnd.
Rep this rnd throughout.

Directions

Cast on 64 sts, join to work in the round.

Cuff & Leg

Work in single rib st until leg measures 6 in. (15 cm) from cast-on edge (or desired length).

Heel

Done in rows as in a flat panel using short-rows on 32 pegs. Follow short-row shaping instructions on page 25 until 12 sts remain unwrapped. End ready for a clockwise row. Continue with the reverse short-row shaping instructions on page 26.

Foot

Done in the round, sole is done in St st, instep continues in single rib st.
Next rnd: k31, p1 *k1, p1; rep from * to the end of rnd.
Repeat last rnd until foot measures 6½ in. (16.5 cm) from back of heel (or desired length).

Toe

Follow short-row shaping as previously done for the heel.
Remove sts from loom as follows:
Place on dpn 1: Sts from pegs 1–32.
Place on dpn 2: Sts from pegs 33–64.
Sts are now prepared to graft close.
Follow grafting instructions to close the toe (see page 17 for illustrated instructions).

Finishing

Weave all yarn tail ends.
Block lightly.

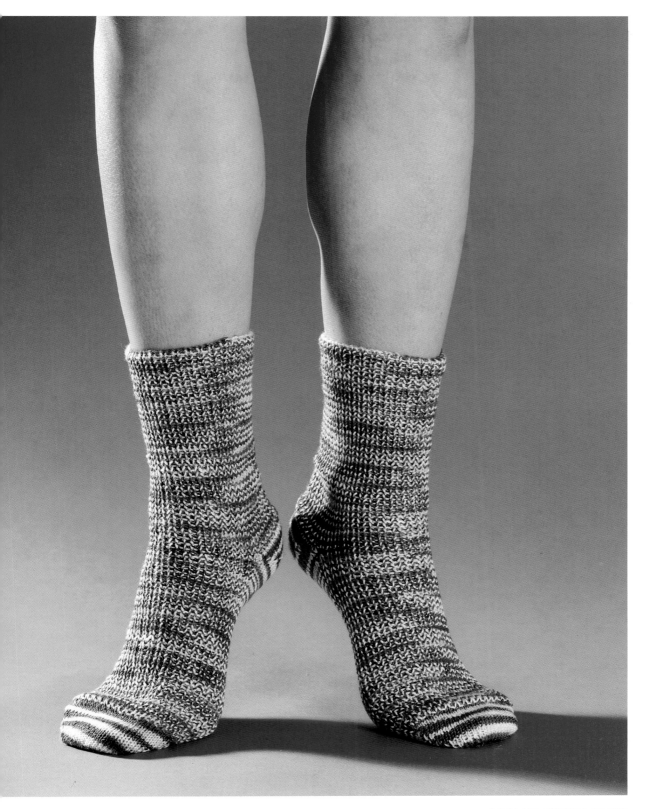

Ribbed sock

The purls break the monotony of stockinette stitch for a more challenging knit. Ribbing provides a perfect fit everytime!

LEVEL 2

MATERIALS

Knitting loom

64 peg extra fine gauge loom. (WonderSock loom was used in this sample.)

Yarn

350–400 yd (320–365 m) of sock weight yarn. (Sample uses Malabrigo sock, 100% superwash merino wool, 440 yd [400 m] per 3½ oz [100 g] in Chocolate Amargo.)

1 SUPER FINE

Tools

Knitting tool
Tapestry needle
2 double pointed needles in size 2 (US)

Gauge

18 sts and 22 rows to 2 in. (5 cm) in St st (knit all rows)

Size

Shown in 8½ in. (21.5 cm) foot circumference.

Adapt

Can be adapted to any other (smaller or larger) loom with a peg multiple of 4.

Pattern note

Read chart from bottom up. Every round is read from right to left.

Stitch pattern:
Modified rib

4 st repeat. Work from chart or use following instructions.

4	3	2	1	
	•		•	1

Key
• Purl
☐ Knit

Rnd 1: k1, p2, k1.
This row forms pattern and is repeated.

Directions

Cast on 64 sts, join to work in the round.

Cuff & leg

Work in Modified rib stitch until leg measures 6 in. (15 cm) from cast-on edge (or desired length).

Heel

Done in rows as in a flat panel using short-rows on 32 pegs. Follow short-row shaping instructions on page 25 until 12 sts remain unwrapped. End ready for a clockwise row. Continue with the reverse short-row shaping instructions on page 26.

Foot

From this point forward, continue working in the round.
Next rnd: k32, continue rib pattern on next 32 sts.
Repeat last round until foot measures desired length (6½ in. [16.5 cm]) from back of heel.

Toe

Follow short row shaping as previously done for the heel.
Remove sts from loom as follows:
Place on dpn 1: Sts from pegs 1–32.
Place on dpn 2: Sts from pegs 33–64.
Sts are now prepared to graft close.
Follow grafting instructions to close the toe (see page 17 for illustrated instructions).

Finishing

Weave all yarn tail ends.
Block lightly.

Classic men's socks

The classic ribbed sock, with a 3x1 rib provides a classy men's trouser sock.

LEVEL 2

MATERIALS

Knitting loom

72 peg extra fine gauge loom. (WonderSock loom was used in this sample.)

Yarn

350–400 yd (320–365 m) of sock weight yarn. (Sample uses Louet Gems 100% merino wool, 185 yd [169 m] per 1¾ oz [50 g] in Linen Gray.)

1 SUPER FINE

Tools

Knitting tool
Tapestry needle
2 double pointed needles size 2 (US)

Gauge

18 sts and 24 rows to 2 in. (5 cm) in St st (knit all rows)

Size

Shown in 9½ in. (24 cm) foot circumference.

Adapt

Can be adapted to any other (smaller or larger) loom with a peg multiple of 4.

Pattern note

Read chart from bottom up. Every round is read from right to left.

Stitch pattern:
3x1 rib stitch pattern

Work from chart or use following instructions.

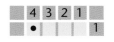

Key

● Purl
☐ Knit

Rnd 1: k3, p1.

Directions

Cast on 72 sts, join to work in the round.

Cuff & leg

Work in 3x1 rib pattern until leg measures 8 in. (20.5 cm) from cast-on edge.

Heel

Done in rows as in a flat panel using short-rows on 36 pegs. Follow short-row shaping instructions on page 25 until 13 sts remain unwrapped. End ready for a clockwise row. Continue with the reverse short-row shaping instructions on page 26.

Foot

Worked in the round. Sole is worked in St st and instep is worked in 3x1 rib pattern.

Next rnd: *k35, p1, work 3x1 rib pattern to the end of rnd.
Repeat last rnd until foot measures 8 in. (20.5 cm) from back of heel (or desired length).

Toe

Follow short-row shaping as previously done for the heel. Remove sts from loom as follows: Place on dpn 1: Sts from pegs 1–36. Place on dpn 2: Sts from pegs 37–72.
Sts are now prepared to graft close. Follow grafting instructions to close the toe (see page 17 for illustrated instructions).

Finishing

Weave all yarn tail ends.
Block lightly.

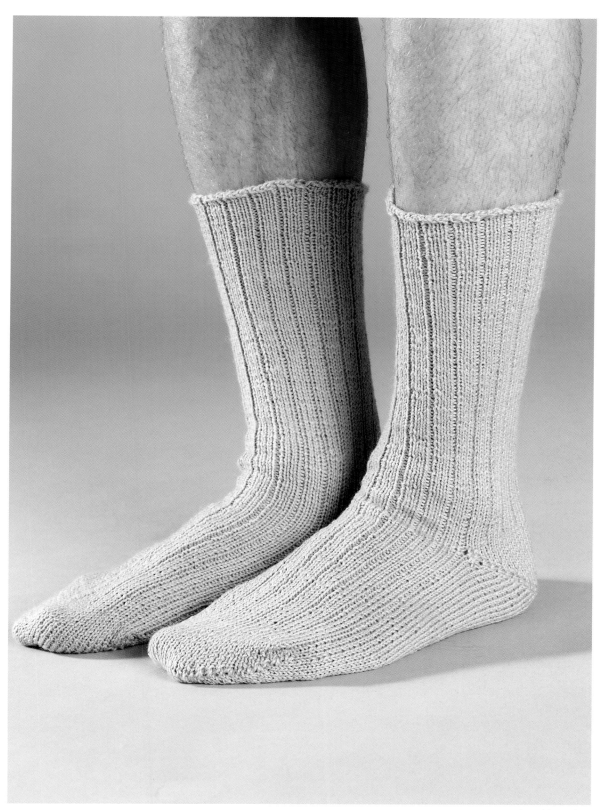

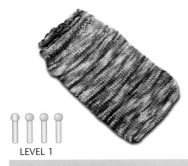

LEVEL 1

ShaSha socks

The perfect sock for a beginner, short in length and all in stockinette stitch, it is the perfect traveling project. The toe shaping is excluded from this pattern to allow for a quick knit. Optional toe shaping instructions are also included.

MATERIALS

Knitting loom

64 peg extra fine gauge loom. (WonderSock loom was used in this sample.)

Yarn

350–400 yd (320–365 m) of sock weight yarn. (Sample uses Sweet Georgia Yarns 100% superwash merino wool 185 yd [170 m] per 1¾ oz [50 g] in Stillwater.)

1 SUPER FINE

Tools

Knitting tool
Tapestry needle
2 double pointed needles size 2 (US)

Gauge

18 sts and 24 rows to 2 in. (5 cm) in St st (knit all rows)

Size

Shown in 8 in. (20.5 cm) foot circumference.

Adapt

Can be adapted to any other (smaller or larger) loom with a peg multiple of 4.

Stitch pattern:
Rib stitch
Rnd 1: *k2, p2; rep from * to the end of rnd.

Directions
Cast on 64 sts, join to work in the round.

Cuff
Work in rib pattern for 1 in. (2.5 cm).

Leg
Work in St st for 1 in. (2.5 cm).

Heel
Done in rows as in a flat panel using short-rows on 32 pegs. Follow short-row shaping instructions on page 25 until 12 sts remain unwrapped. End ready for a clockwise row. Continue with the reverse short-row shaping instructions on page 26.

Foot
Worked in the round in St st until foot measures desired length (9 in. [23 cm] for our sample).

Toe
No shaping
Remove sts from loom as follows:
Place on dpn 1: Sts from pegs 1–32.
Place on dpn 1: Sts from pegs 33–64.
Sts are now prepared to graft close. Follow grafting instructions to close the toe (see page 17 for illustrated instructions).

Shaped option
Follow short-row shaping as previously done for the heel.
Remove sts from loom as follows:
Place on dpn 1: Sts from pegs 1–32.
Place on dpn 1: Sts from pegs 33–64.
Sts are now prepared to graft close. Follow grafting instructions to close the toe (see page 17 for illustrated instructions).

Finishing
Weave all yarn tail ends.
Block lightly.

PART II
Textured socks

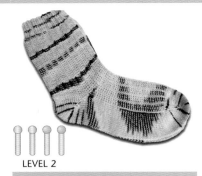

LEVEL 2

Guppy socks

This wonderful sock yarn called for a stitch pattern that was simple yet had a twist. The slipped stitch with a background of reverse stockinette allows the beauty of the yarn to come through.

MATERIALS

Knitting loom

64 peg extra fine gauge loom. (The WonderSock loom was used in this sample.)

Yarn

350–400 yd (320–365 m) of sock weight yarn. (Sample uses Sweet Georgia 100% superwash merino wool fingering [handpainted] 185 yd [169 m] per 1¾ oz [50 g] in Rainforest.)

1 SUPER FINE

Tools

Knitting tool
Tapestry needle
2 double pointed needles size 2 (US)

Gauge

18 sts and 20 rows to 2 in. (5 cm) in St st (knit all rows)

Size

Shown in 8½ in. (21.5 cm) foot circumference.

Adapt

Can be adapted to any other (smaller or larger) loom with a peg multiple of 4.

Stitch pattern:
Slipped stitch
Rnd1: p3, sl1.
Rnd2: Knit 4 st and 2 row repeat.

Directions
Cast on 64sts, join to work in the round.

Cuff
Rnds 1–14: *k2, p2; rep from * to the end of round.

Leg
Next rnd: Start and work in slip pattern until leg measures 6 in. (15 cm) from cast-on edge (or desired length). End on a rnd 15.

Heel
Done in rows as in a flat panel using short-rows on 32 pegs. Follow short-row shaping instructions on page 25 until 12 sts remain unwrapped. End ready for a clockwise row. Continue with the reverse short-row shaping instructions on page 26.

Foot
Worked in the round. Sole is worked in St st, instep continues in reverse slip pattern as follows:
Next rnd: Knit.
**Next rnd: k31, sl1, *p3, sl1; rep from * to the end of rnd.
Next rnd: Knit.**
Rep from ** to ** until sole measures 2 in. (5 cm) less than desired length.

Toe
Follow short-row shaping as previously done for the heel. Remove sts from loom as follows:
Place on dpn 1: Sts from pegs 1–32.
Place on dpn 2: Sts from pegs 33–64.
Sts are now prepared to graft close. Follow grafting instructions to close the toe (see page 17 for illustrated instructions).

Finishing
Weave all yarn tail ends.
Block lightly.

Borderline socks

This unisex pattern has attractive diamond detail to the cuff, making it a great idea for a gift.

LEVEL 2

MATERIALS

Knitting loom

72 peg extra fine gauge loom. (The WonderSock loom was used in this sample.)

Yarn

350–400 yd (320–365 m) of sock weight yarn. (Sample uses Berroco Comfort Sock, 50% Super Fine Nylon 50% Super Fine Acrylic, 447 yd [412 m] per 3½ oz [100 g] in Navy.)

1 SUPER FINE

Tools

Knitting tool
Tapestry needle
2 double pointed needles size 2 (US).

Gauge

18 sts and 24 rows to 2 in. (5 cm) in St st (knit all rows)

Size

Shown in 10 in. (25.5 cm) foot circumference.

Adapt

Can be adapted to any other (smaller or larger) loom with a peg multiple of 9.

Stitch pattern:
2x2 rib

*k2, p2: rep from * to end of rnd.

9 8 7 6 5 4 3 2 1	
	9
• • •	8
• • • • •	7
• • • • • • •	6
• • • • • • • • •	5
• • • • • • •	4
• • • • •	3
• • •	2
•	1

Key
• Purl
  Knit

Directions

Cast on 72 sts, join to work in the round.

Cuff

Work 1 in. (2.5 cm) in 2x2 rib.

Leg

Rnds 1 and 2: Knit.
Rnds 3 and 4: Purl.
Rnds 5 and 6: Knit.
Rnds 7–15: Follow diamond pattern.
Rnds 16 and 17: Knit.
Rnds 18 and 19: Purl.
Rnd 20: Knit.

Repeat rnd 20 until item measures 7½ in. (19 cm), or desired length, from cast-on edge.

Heel

Done in rows as in a flat panel using short-rows on 36 pegs. Follow short-row shaping instructions on page 25 until 14 sts remain unwrapped. End ready for a clockwise row. Continue with the reverse short-row shaping instructions on page 26.

Foot

Worked in the round in St st (knit every round). Work in St st until foot measures 2 in. (5 cm) less than desired length.

Toe

Follow short-row shaping as previously done for the heel. Remove sts from loom as follows: Place on dpn 1: Sts from pegs 1–36. Place on dpn 2: Sts from pegs 37–72.
Sts are now prepared to graft close. Follow grafting instructions to close the toe (see page 17 for illustrated instructions).

Finishing

Weave all yarn tail ends.
Block lightly.

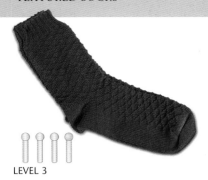

LEVEL 3

Robin's brocade socks

A few purls and knits placed at strategic locations create the most impressive texture of diagonals. The stitch pattern is simple however do not blink as you may miss a row!

MATERIALS

Knitting loom

64 peg extra fine gauge loom. (WonderSock loom was used in this sample.)

Yarn

350–400 yd (320–365 m) of fingering weight yarn. (Sample uses Berroco Comfort Sock, 50% Super Fine Nylon 50% Super Fine Acrylic, 447 yd [412 m] per 3½ oz [100 g] in Burgundy.)

1 SUPER FINE

Tools

Knitting tool
Tapestry needle
2 double pointed needles size 2 (US)

Gauge

18 sts and 24 rows to 2 in. (5 cm) in St st (knit all rows)

Size

Shown in 8½ in. (21.5 cm) foot circumference.

Adapt

Can be adapted to any other (smaller or larger) loom with a peg multiple of 8.

Stitch pattern:
2x2 rib
*k2, p2: rep from * to end of rnd.

Robin's brocade pattern
Read chart from bottom up. Every round is read from right to left. Work from chart or follow written directions.

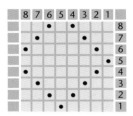

Key
● Purl
☐ Knit

Rnd 1: k4, p1, k3.
Rnd 2: k3, p1, k1, p1, k2.
Rnd 3: k2, p1, k3, p1, k1.
Rnd 4: k1, p1, k5, p1.
Rnd 5: p1, k7.
Rnd 6: k1, p1, k5, p1.
Rnd 7: k2, p1, k3, p1, k1.
Rnd 8: k3, p1, k1, p1, k2.
8 st and 8 row repeat.

Directions
Cast on 64 sts, join to work in the round.

Cuff
Work 1½ in. (4 cm) in 2x2 rib pattern.

Leg
Next rnd: Start and work Robin's brocade pattern (chart repeat 8 times around the loom) and work in pattern until item measures

7 in. (18 cm) from cast-on edge. End on a rnd 1.

Heel
Done in rows as in a flat panel using short-rows on 32 pegs. Follow short-row shaping instructions on page 25 until 12 sts remain unwrapped. End ready for a clockwise row. Continue with the reverse short-row shaping instructions on page 26.

Foot
Worked in the round. Sole is worked in St st, upper section of foot continues in brocade pattern.
Rnd 1–4: k32, continue brocade pattern to the end of rnd.
Rnd 5: p1, k31, continue brocade pattern to the end of rnd.
Rnd 6–8: k32, continue brocade pattern to the end of rnd.*

Repeat from * to * until item measures desired length from back of heel minus 2 in. (5 cm) (7 in. [18 cm] for our sample.)
Next rnd: k32, work rnd 1 of brocade pattern to the end of rnd.

Toe
Follow short-row shaping as previously done for the heel.
Remove sts from loom as follows:
Place on dpn 1: Sts from pegs 32–1.
Place on dpn 2: Sts from pegs 33–64.
Sts are now prepared to graft close.

Follow grafting instructions to close the toe (see page 17 for illustrated instructions).

Finishing
Weave all yarn tail ends.
Block lightly.

Seeded rib socks

The seeded rib gives a basic ribbed sock extra spice. The seeded rib creates a nice and dense textured fabric.

LEVEL 2

MATERIALS

Knitting loom

72 peg extra fine gauge loom. (WonderSock loom was used in this sample.)

Yarn

350–400 yd (320–365 m) of sock weight yarn. (Sample uses ShiBuiKnits 100% superwash merino, 190 yd [175 m] per 1¾ oz [50 g] in Seaweed.)

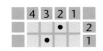

1 SUPER FINE

Tools

Knitting tool
Tapestry needle
2 double pointed needles size 2 (US)

Gauge

18 sts and 22 rows to 2 in. (5 cm) in St st (knit all rows)

Size

Shown in 9½ in. (24 cm) foot circumference.

Adapt

Can be adapted to any other (smaller or larger) loom with a peg multiple of 4.

Stitch patterns:

Single rib stitch

Rnd 1: *k1, p1; rep from * to the end of rnd.
Rep rnd 1.

Seeded rib stitch

Read chart from bottom up. Every round is read from right to left. Work from chart or follow written directions.

Key
• Purl
☐ Knit

Rnd 1: k1, p1, k1.
Rnd 2: k2, p1, k2.
Pattern is 4 st x 2 row repeat.

Directions

Cast on 72 sts, join to work in the round.

Cuff

Work in single rib pattern for 2 in. (5 cm).

Leg

Next rnd: Start and work seeded rib pattern (the pattern repeats 16 times on a round) until leg measures 8 in. (20.5 cm) from cast-on edge (or desired length). End on a row 2.

Heel

Done in rows as in a flat panel using short-rows on 36 pegs. Follow short-row shaping instructions on page 25 until 13 sts remain unwrapped. End ready for a clockwise row. Continue with the reverse short-row shaping instructions on page 26.

Foot

Worked in the round. Sole is worked in St st and instep is worked in seeded rib pattern.
Next rnd: k36, work seeded rib pattern on next 36 sts.
Work in st st and seeded Rib pattern as set until foot measures 8 in. (20.5 cm) from back of heel (or desired length). End on a row 2.

Toe

Follow short-row shaping as previously done for the heel. Remove sts from loom as follows:
Place on dpn 1: Sts from pegs 1–36.
Place on dpn 2: Sts from pegs 37–72.
Sts are now prepared to graft close. Follow grafting instructions to close the toe (see page 17 for illustrated instructions).

Finishing

Weave all yarn tail ends.
Block lightly.

Garter stitch

Grab your favorite yarn, be it variegated or solid and take it for a spin with this easy sock pattern.

LEVEL 2

MATERIALS

Knitting loom

64 peg extra fine gauge loom. (WonderSock loom was used in this sample.)

Yarn

350–400 yd (320–365 m) of sock weight yarn. (Sample uses ShiBuiKnits 100% superwash merino, 190 yd [175 m] per 1¾ oz [50 g] in Earth.)

1 SUPER FINE

Tools

Knitting tool
Tapestry needle
2 double pointed needles size 2 (US)

Gauge

18 sts and 22 rows to 2 in. (5 cm) in St st (knit all rows)

Size

Shown in 8 in. (20 cm) foot circumference.

Adapt

Can be adapted to any sized knitting loom.

Tip

A crochet hook makes picking the sts easier.

Stitch pattern:
Garter stitch (g-st)

Rnd 1: Knit.
Rnd 2: Purl.
Rep rnds 1 and 2 to create 1 g-st ridge.

Directions

Cast on 36 sts with e-wrap cast-on.

Garter stitch cuff

Work a flat panel in g-st for 6 in. (15 cm)—approximately 128 rows. Bind off with basic bind-off method. Join cast-on sts with bind off edge (graft the cast-on edge to bind off edge).

Leg

Pick up 64 sts around the edge of the g-st cuff (if you worked 128 rows, you will pick up at every other g-st ridge).
Rnds 1–10: Knit.

Heel

Done in rows as in a flat panel using short-rows on 32 pegs. Follow short-row shaping instructions on page 25 until 12 sts remain unwrapped. End ready for a clockwise row. Continue with the reverse short-row shaping instructions on page 26.

Foot

Worked in the round.
Continue working in the round in St st until foot measures 7 in. (18 cm) from back of heel (or desired length).

Toe

Follow short-row shaping as previously done for the heel. Remove sts from loom as follows:
Place on dpn 1: Sts from pegs 1–32.
Place on dpn 2: Sts from pegs 33–64.
Sts are now prepared to graft close. Follow grafting instructions to close the toe (see page 17 for illustrated instructions).

Finishing

Weave all yarn tail ends.
Block lightly.

Baskets

An easy basketweave pattern around the cuff makes this pattern interesting and fast to knit.

LEVEL 2

MATERIALS

Knitting loom

64 peg extra fine gauge loom. (WonderSock loom was used in this sample.)

Yarn

300–350 yd (274–320 m) of sock weight yarn. (Sample uses Scout's Swag, 100% superwash merino, 370–400yd [338–365 m] per 3½ oz [100 g] in Pear.)

1 SUPER FINE

Tools

Knitting tool
Tapestry needle
2 double pointed needles size 2 (US)

Gauge

18 sts and 24 rows to 2 in. (5 cm) in St st (knit all rows)

Size

Shown in 8½ in. (21.5 cm) foot circumference.

Adapt

Can be adapted to any other (smaller or larger) loom with a peg multiple of 8.

Stitch pattern: Basket weave

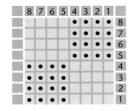

Key
● Purl
☐ Knit

Rnd 1–4: k4, p4.
Rnd 5–8: p4, k4.
8 st (+4) x 8 row repeat.

Directions

Cast on 64 sts, join to work in the round.

Cuff & leg

Rnds 1–8: Work in basket weave to the end of round.
Repeat last 8 rnds until cuff and leg measure 4 in. (10 cm) from cast-on edge.

Heel

Done in rows as in a flat panel using short-rows on 32 pegs. Follow short-row shaping instructions on page 25 until 12 sts remain unwrapped. End ready for a clockwise row. Continue with the reverse short-row shaping instructions on page 26.

Foot

From this point forward, continue working in the round.
Next rnd: Knit.
Repeat last rnd until foot measures desired length (6½ in. [16.5 cm]) from back of heel.

Toe

Follow short-row shaping as previously done for the heel. Remove sts from loom as follows: Place on dpn 1: Sts from pegs 1–32. Place on dpn 2: Sts from pegs 33–64.
Sts are now prepared to graft close. Follow grafting instructions to close the toe (see page 17 for illustrated instructions).

Finishing

Weave all yarn tail ends.
Block lightly.

Spiraling tubes

The spiraling tubes are the most basic project you will find in this book. It is the basic tube sock with a twist!

LEVEL 2

MATERIALS

Knitting loom

64 peg extra fine gauge loom. (WonderSock loom was used in this sample.)

Yarn

350–400 yd (320–365 m) of sock weight yarn. (Sample uses ShiBuiKnits 100% superwash merino fingering weight, 191 yd [175 m] per 1¾ oz [50 g] in 51305.)

2 FINE

Tools

Knitting tool
Tapestry needle
2 double pointed needles size 2 (US)
Cable needle

Gauge

18 sts and 24 rows to 2 in. (5 cm) in St st (knit all rows)

Size

Shown in 8 in. (20.5 cm) foot circumference.

Adapt

Can be adapted to any other (smaller or larger) loom with a peg multiple of 4.

Pattern note

Read chart from bottom up. Every round is read from right to left.

Stitch pattern:

Work from chart or use following instructions.

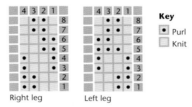

Right leg   Left leg

Key
• Purl
□ Knit

Right leg

Rnd 1: (RS) k2, p2.
Rnd 2: k2, p2.
Rnds 3 and 4: p1, k2, p1.
Rnds 5 and 6: p2, k2.
Rnds 7 and 8: k1, p2, k1.

Left leg

Rnd 1: (RS) p2, k2.
Rnd 2: p2, k2.
Rnds 3 and 4: p1, k2, p1.
Rnds 5 and 6: k2, p2.
Rnds 7 and 8: k1, p2, k1.

Both legs

Rnds 1–8 form pattern and are repeated throughout.

Directions

Cast on 64 sts, join to work in the round.

Right leg

Rnds 1–8: Work in spiraling rib pattern for right leg.
Repeat pattern until entire tube measures 12 in. (30.5 cm) in length.

Toe

Move every loop from the odd pegs over to the neighboring peg (1 to 2, 3 to 4, etc.) Every other peg is empty and every other peg has 2 loops on it. Treat both loops as though they were one.
Next rnd: Knit.

Bind off

Cut yarn leaving a 2-yd (2-m) tail. Thread tapestry needle with yarn coming from sock, bind off with gather bind-off method (see page 16 for illustrated instructions).

Left leg

Repeat instructions for right leg except follow left leg rib pattern.

Finishing

Weave in all ends (see page 27).

Moss stitch

The moss stitch pattern goes around the cuff to provide with a nice and dense fabric to keep you warm.

LEVEL 2

MATERIALS

Knitting loom

64 peg extra fine gauge loom. (WonderSock loom was used in this sample.)

Yarn

350–400 yd (320–365 m) of sock weight yarn. (Sample uses Malabrigo sock 100% superwash merino wool 440 yd [402 m] per 3½ oz [100 g] in Violet.)

1 SUPER FINE

Tools

Knitting tool
Tapestry needle
2 double pointed needles size 2 (US)

Gauge

18 sts and 21 rows to 2 in. (5 cm) in St st (knit all rows)

Size

Shown in 8½ in (21.5 cm) foot circumference.

Adapt

Can be adapted to any other (smaller or larger) loom with a peg multiple of 2.

Stitch pattern:
Moss stitch pattern

Read chart from bottom up. Every round is read from right to left. Work from chart or follow directions.

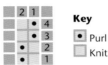

Key
● Purl
□ Knit

Rnds 1 and 2: k1, p1.
Rnds 3 and 4: p1, k1.

Directions

Cast on 64 sts, join to work in the round.

Cuff & leg

Start and work moss stitch pattern until leg measures 4 in. (10 cm) from cast-on edge (or desired length).

Heel

Done in rows as in a flat panel using short-rows on 32 pegs. Follow short-row shaping instructions on page 25 until 12 sts remain unwrapped. End ready for a clockwise row. Continue with the reverse short-row shaping instructions on page 26.

Foot

Worked in the round in St st. Knit until foot measures 6½ in. (16.5 cm) from back of heel.

Toe

Follow short-row shaping as previously done for the heel. Remove sts from loom as follows: Place on dpn 1: Sts from pegs 32–1. Place on dpn 2: Sts from pegs 33–64.
Sts are now prepared to graft close. Follow grafting instructions to close the toe (see page 17 for illustrated instructions).

Finishing

Weave all yarn tail ends. Block lightly.

Seascape melody

The yarn in this pattern has a subtle color quality. It changes color so you don't have to!

LEVEL 2

MATERIALS

Knitting loom

64 peg extra fine gauge knitting loom. (WonderSock loom was used in this sample.)

Yarn

350–400 yd (320–365 m) of sock weight yarn. (Sample uses ShiBuiKnits 100% Superwash merino, 190 yd [175 m] per 1¾ oz [50 g], in Manblue S350.)

1 SUPER FINE

Tools

Knitting tool
Tapestry needle
2 double pointed needles size 2 (US)

Gauge

18 sts and 24 rows to 2 in. (5 cm) in St st (knit all rows)

Size

Shown in 8 in. (20.5 cm) foot circumference.

Adapt

Can be adapted to any other (smaller or larger) loom with a peg multiple of 4.

Stitch pattern:
Welted rib pattern

Read chart from bottom up. Every round is read from right to left. Work from chart or follow written directions.

Rnd 1: k1, p2, k1.
Rnd 2: k4.
4st and 2 row repeat.

Key
● Purl
□ Knit

Directions

Cast on 64 sts, join to work in the round.

Cuff

Rnd 1: *k1, p2, k1; rep from * to the end of rnd.
Repeat rnd 1 until cuff measures 2 in. (5 cm) from cast-on edge.

Leg

Rnds 1–2: Work welted rib pattern (the pattern repeats 16 times on a round). Repeat rnds 1–2 until leg measures 6 in. (15 cm) from cast-on edge (or desired length). End on a row 2.

Heel

Done in rows as in a flat panel using short-rows on 32 pegs. Follow short-row shaping instructions on page 25 until 12 sts remain unwrapped. Continue with the reverse short-row shaping instructions on page 26.

Foot

Worked in the round. Sole is worked in St st, instep continues in rib pattern as follows:
Next rnd: k32, work rib pattern until end of rnd.
Continue in st st and rib pattern as set until foot measures 7 in. (18 cm) from back of heel (or desired length).

Toe

Follow short row shaping as previously done for the heel. Remove sts from loom as follows:
Place on dpn 1: Sts from pegs 1–32.
Place on dpn 2: Sts from pegs 33–64.
Sts are now prepared to graft close. Follow grafting instructions to close the toe (see page 17 for illustrated instructions).

Finishing

Weave all yarn tail ends. Block lightly.

Slouch socks

Wear them pulled up or slouch them down—either way, they will look fabulous.

LEVEL 2

MATERIALS

Knitting loom

64 peg extra fine gauge loom. (WonderSock loom was used in this sample.)

Yarn

350–400 yd (320–365 m) of sock weight yarn. (Sample uses Malabrigo sock 100% superwash merino wool 440 yd [402 m] per 3½ oz [100 g] in Lettuce.)

1 SUPER FINE

Tools

Knitting tool
Tapestry needle
2 double pointed needles size 2 (US)

Gauge

18 sts and 21 rows to 2 in. (5 cm) St st (knit all rows)

Size

Shown in 8½ in. (21.5 cm) foot circumference.

Adapt

Can be adapted to another (smaller or larger) loom with any peg multiple.

Pattern note

Read chart from bottom up. Every round is read from right to left.

Stitch pattern: Slouch

Key
● Purl
☐ Knit

Rnds 1–2: Knit.
Rnds 3–6: Purl.
These 6 rows form pattern and are repeated.

Directions

Cast on 64 sts, join to work in the round.

Cuff

Rnd 1: Knit.
Rnd 2: Purl.
Rep rnd 1 and 2 until cuff measures 1½ in. (4 cm) from cast-on edge.

Leg

Next rnd: Start and work slouch pattern 1–6 until leg measures 6 in. (15 cm) from cast-on edge (or desired length). End on a row 6.

Heel

Done in rows as in a flat panel using short-rows on 32 pegs. Follow short-row shaping instructions on page 25 until 12 sts remain unwrapped. End ready for a clockwise row. Continue with the reverse short-row shaping instructions on page 26.

Foot

Worked in the round. Sole is worked in St st, instep is continued in slouch pattern as follows:
Next rnd: k32, work slouch pattern over next 32 sts.
Continue in St st and slouch pattern as set until foot measures 7 in. (18 cm) from back of heel (or desired length). End on a rnd 1 or rnd 2 of slouch pattern.

Toe

Follow short-row shaping as previously done for the heel. Remove sts from loom as follows: Place on dpn 1: Sts from pegs 1–32. Place on dpn 2: Sts from pegs 33–64.

Sts are now prepared to graft close. Follow grafting instructions to close the toe (see page 17 for illustrated instructions).

Finishing

Weave all yarn tail ends. Block lightly.

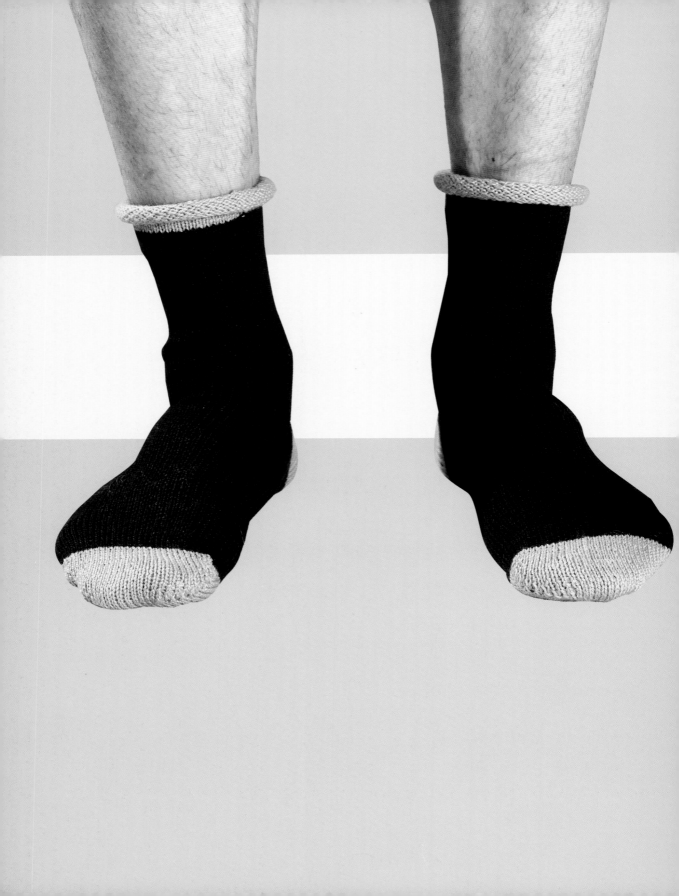

PART III
Colorwork socks

Snow

When the weather gets cold, match your socks to the climate by wearing these cozy socks with lovely patterned cuffs.

LEVEL 4

MATERIALS

Knitting loom

64 peg extra fine gauge loom. (WonderSock loom was used in this sample.)

Yarn

350–400 yd (320–365 m) of sock weight yarn. (Sample uses Louet Gems 100% merino wool, 185 yd [169 m] per 1¾ oz [50 g].) 2 x skeins Bright Blue. 1 x skein Pure White.

1 SUPER FINE

Tools

Knitting tool
Tapestry needle
2 double pointed needles size 2 (US)

Gauge

18 sts and 22 rows to 2 in. (5 cm) in St st (knit all rows)

Size

Shown in 8½ in. (21.5 cm) foot circumference.

Abbreviations

MC is Bright Blue yarn.
CC is Pure White yarn.

Adapt

Can be adapted to any other loom with a peg multiple of 16.

Pattern note

Stranding: When traveling with the yarn, if the distance between color changes is not greater than 4 sts the yarn can be left at the back of the work until it is needed. When needed, pick it up and work with it as indicated in the pattern. This process is called stranding and it creates a series of floats at the back of the work.

Stitch patterns:

Rib stitch

Rnd 1: *k2, p2: rep from * to the end of rnd.
Repeat rnd 1.

Snow

Read the chart from bottom up. Right to left every round. Work pattern from chart.

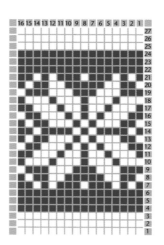

Key
☐ CC
■ MC

Directions

With MC, cast on 64 sts, join to work in the round.

Cuff

Rnds 1–6: *k2, p2; rep from * to the end of rnd.

Leg

Next 3 rnds: Knit. Join CC.
Next 27 rnds: Work snow chart, change colors as indicated in chart. When chart is completed, cut CC leaving a 6 in. (15 cm) tail and continue with MC.
Work in St st until leg measures 6 in. (15 cm) from cast-on edge (or desired length).
Join CC, do not cut MC.

Heel

Done completely in CC in rows as in a flat panel using short-rows on 32 pegs. Follow short-row shaping instructions on page 25 until 12 sts remain unwrapped. End ready for a clockwise row. Continue with the reverse short-row shaping instructions on page 26. Cut CC leaving a 6-in. (15-cm) tail. Continue with MC.

Foot

Worked in MC, in the round. Continue working in the round in St st until foot measures desired length from back of heel (6½ in [16.5 cm] for our sample). Cut MC leaving a 6-in. (15-cm) tail, join CC.

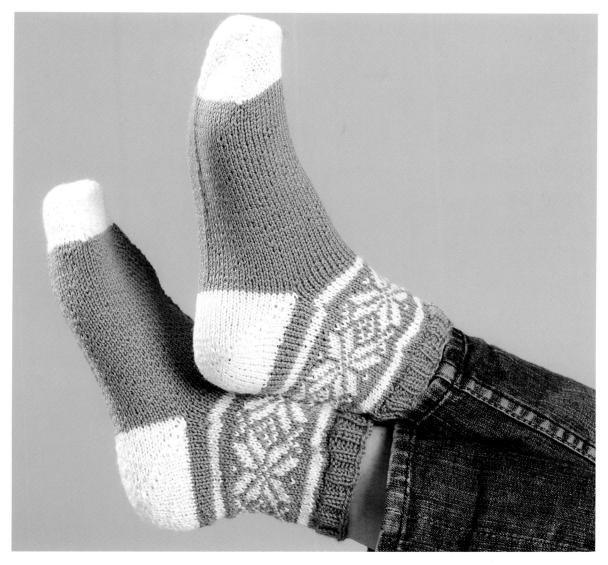

Toe

Worked in CC.

Follow short-row shaping as previously done for the heel.

Remove sts from loom as follows:

Place on dpn 1: Sts from pegs 1–32.

Place on dpn 2: Sts from pegs 33–64.

Sts are now prepared to graft close. Follow grafting instructions to close the toe (see page 17 for illustrated instructions).

Finishing

Weave all yarn tail ends.

Block lightly.

Golden heels and toes

Step into a little pool of gold and get your toes colored gold. Why should men's socks be boring?

LEVEL 2

MATERIALS

Knitting loom

64 peg extra fine gauge loom (WonderSock loom was used in this sample.)

Yarn

350–400 yd (320–365 m) of sock weight yarn. (Sample uses Louet Gems 100% Merino wool, 185 yd [169 m] per 1¾ oz [50g].) 2 x skeins Indigo. 1 x skein Goldenrod.

1 SUPER FINE

Tools

Knitting tool
Tapestry needle
2 double pointed needles size 2 (US)

Gauge

18 sts and 24 rows to 2 in. (5 cm) in St st (knit all rows).

Size

Shown in 8½ in. (21.5 cm) foot circumference.

Abbreviations

MC is Indigo yarn.
CC is Goldenrod yarn.

Adapt

Can be adapted to another loom with any peg multiple.

Directions

With CC, cast on 64 sts, join to work in the round.

Cuff

Rnd 1–20: Knit.
Cut CC and attach MC.

Leg

With MC, work in St st until leg measures 6 in. (15 cm) from cast-on edge.

Heel

Attach CC and work heel in CC (note: do not cut MC). Done in rows as in a flat panel using short-rows on 32 pegs. Follow short-row shaping instructions on page 25 until 12 sts remain unwrapped. End ready for a clockwise row. Continue with the reverse short-row shaping instructions on page 26.
Cut CC leaving a 6 in. (15 cm) tail.

Foot

Worked in the round with MC. Sole and foot is worked in St st. Continue working in St st until foot measures desired length (7 in. [18 cm] for our sample).

Toe

Cut MC leaving a 6 in. (15 cm) tail, join CC and work heel in CC.
Follow short-row shaping as previously done for the heel.
Remove sts from loom as follows:
Place on dpn 1: Sts from pegs 32–1.
Place on dpn 2: Sts from pegs 33–64.

Sts are now prepared to graft close. Follow grafting instructions to close the toe (see page 17 for illustrated instructions).

Finishing

Weave all yarn tail ends.
Block lightly.

Horizontal striped socks

This retro striped sock, easy to create, will bring back memories of old school sports teams.

LEVEL 2

MATERIALS

Knitting loom

64 peg extra fine gauge knitting loom (WonderSock loom was used in this sample.)

Yarn

350–400 yd (320–365 m) of sock weight yarn. (Sample uses Louet Gems 100% merino wool, 185 yd [169 m] per 1¾ oz [50 g].)
1 x skein Burgundy.
1 x skein Goldenrod.

1 SUPER FINE

Tools

Knitting tool
Tapestry needle
2 double pointed needles size 2 (US)

Size

Shown in 8½ in. (21.5 cm) foot circumference.

Gauge

18 sts and 24 rows to 2 in. (5 cm) in St st (knit all rows)

Abbreviations

MC is Burgundy yarn.
CC is Goldenrod yarn.

Adapt

Can be adapted to another loom with any peg multiple.

Stitch patterns:
Stripe

Work 4 rnds with CC, pick up MC. Work 4 rnds of MC, pick up CC. Repeat last 8 rnds for stripe pattern.

Rib stitch

Rnd 1: *k2, p2: rep from * to the end of round
Repeat rnd 1.

Directions

With MC, cast on 64 sts, join to work in the round.

Cuff

Work in rib stitch for 1½ in (4 cm).

Leg

Join CC, and continue with CC (do not cut MC, just let it drop to the side).
Work in stripe pattern until leg measures 6–6½ in. (15–16.5 cm) from cast-on edge (end on 4th row of MC, do not cut CC).

Heel

Done completely in MC in rows as in a flat panel using short-rows on 32 pegs. Follow short-row shaping instructions on page 25 until 12 sts remain unwrapped. End ready for a clockwise row. Continue with the reverse short-row shaping instructions on page 26.

Foot

Worked in the round.
Work in stripe pattern as before until foot measures desired length (7 in. [18 cm] for our sample). Cut CC, leaving a 5-in. (12.5-cm) tail.

Toe

Done completely in MC, follow
short-row shaping as for the heel.
Remove sts from loom as follows:
Place on dpn 1: Sts from pegs 32–1.
Place on dpn 2: Sts from pegs
33–64.
The sts are now prepared to graft
together. Follow grafting
instructions to close the toe (see
page 17 for illustrated instructions).

Finishing

Weave in all yarn tail ends.
Block lightly.

Blooms for Bethany

Named after one of my close loomy friends, these socks remind me of her cheerful disposition.

LEVEL 4

MATERIALS

Knitting loom

72 peg extra fine gauge loom. (WonderSock loom used here.)

Yarn

350–400 yd (320–365 m) of sock weight yarn. (Sample uses Louet Gems 100% merino wool, 185 yd [169 m] per 1¾ oz [50 g].)
2 x skeins in Pure White.
1 x skeins in Willow.
1 x skeins in Pink Panther.

1 SUPER FINE

Tools

Knitting tool
Tapestry needle
2 double pointed needles size 2 (US)

Gauge

18 sts and 22 rows to 2 in. (5 cm) in St st (knit all rows)

Size

Shown in size 8½ in. (21.5 cm) circumference.

Abbreviations

A is Pure White yarn.
B is Willow yarn.
C is Pink Panther yarn.

Adapt

Looms with a peg multiple of 18.

Pattern note

Read the chart from bottom up. Right to left every round.

Stitch pattern:
Rib stitch

Rnd 1: *k2; p2; rep from * to the end of rnd.
Repeat rnd 1.

Directions

Cast on 72 sts, join to work in the round.

Cuff

Work in rib stitch for 1 in. (2.5 cm).

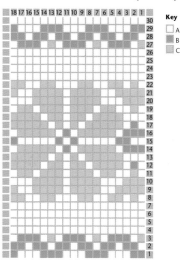

Key
□ A
▨ B
▧ C

Leg

Rnds 1–5: Knit.
Next 30 rnds: Follow ribbon and flowers chart. When chart has been completed, cut B and C leaving 6-in. (15-cm) tails and continue with A only.

Continue in St st until leg measures 6½ in. (16.5 cm) from cast-on edge.

Heel

Done in rows as in a flat panel using short-rows on 36 pegs. Follow short-row shaping instructions on page 25 until 14 sts remain unwrapped. End ready for a clockwise row. Continue with the reverse short-row shaping instructions on page 26.

Foot

Worked in the round. Sole and instep are worked in St st until foot measures desired length (7 in. [18 cm] for our sample).

Toe

Follow short-row shaping as previously done for the heel. Remove sts from loom as follows: Place on dpn 1: Sts from pegs 1–32. Place on dpn 2: Sts from pegs 37–72.
Sts are now prepared to graft close. Follow grafting instructions to close the toe (see page 17 for illustrated instructions).

Finishing

Weave all yarn tail ends.
Block lightly.

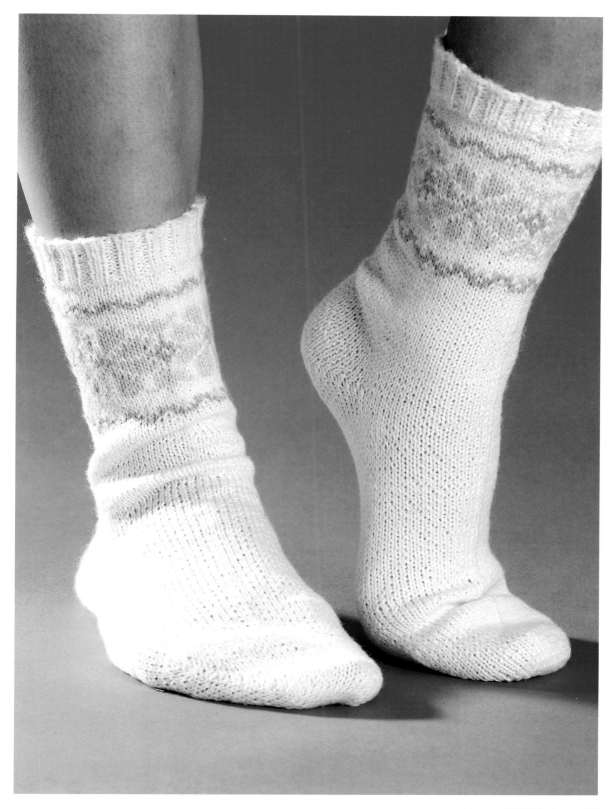

Tennis socks

Whether you choose to play tennis in them or not, these light socks are perfect for day-to-day wear.

LEVEL 4

Stitch pattern:
Single rib stitch
Rnd 1: *k1, p1; rep from * to the end of rnd.
Rep rnd 1.

Directions
With MC, cast on 64 sts, join to work in the round.

Cuff
Rnds 1–8: Work in single rib pattern, drop MC.
Rnds 9–10: Join CC, and work in single rib pattern, drop CC.
Rnd 11: Pick up MC, work in single rib pattern, drop CC.
Rnd 12–13: Pick up CC, work in single rib pattern, cut CC and continue working in MC.
Rnds 14–21: Pick up MC, work in single rib pattern.

Leg
With MC, work in St st (knit every rnd) for 1 in. (2.5 cm).

Heel
Done completely in MC in rows as in a flat panel using short-rows on 32 pegs. Follow short-row shaping instructions on page 25 until 12 sts remain unwrapped. End ready for a clockwise row. Continue with the reverse short-row shaping instructions on page 26.

Foot
Worked in the round. Sole and foot is worked in St st. Continue working in St st until foot measures 5 rows less than desired length from back of heel (6 in. [15 cm] for our sample). Next 5 rows as follows:
Rnds 1–2: Join CC, and work in Single Rib pattern, drop CC.
Rnd 3: Pick up MC, work in Single Rib pattern, drop MC.
Rnd 4–5: Pick up CC, work in Single Rib pattern, cut CC and continue working in MC.

MATERIALS

Knitting loom

64 peg extra fine gauge knitting loom. (WonderSock loom was used in this sample.)

Yarn

350–400 yd (320–365 m) of sock weight yarn. (Sample uses Louet Gems 100% merino wool, 185 yd [169 m] per 1¾ oz [50 g].)
1 x skein in Pure White.
1 x skein Bright Blue.

1 SUPER FINE

Tools

Knitting tool
Tapestry needle
2 double pointed needles size 2 (US)

Gauge

18 sts and 24 rows to 2 in. (5cm) in St st (knit all rows)

Size

Shown in 8½ in (21.5 cm) foot circumference.

Abbreviations

MC is Pure White yarn.
CC is Bright Blue yarn.

Adapt

Can be adapted to any other loom with a peg multiple of 2.

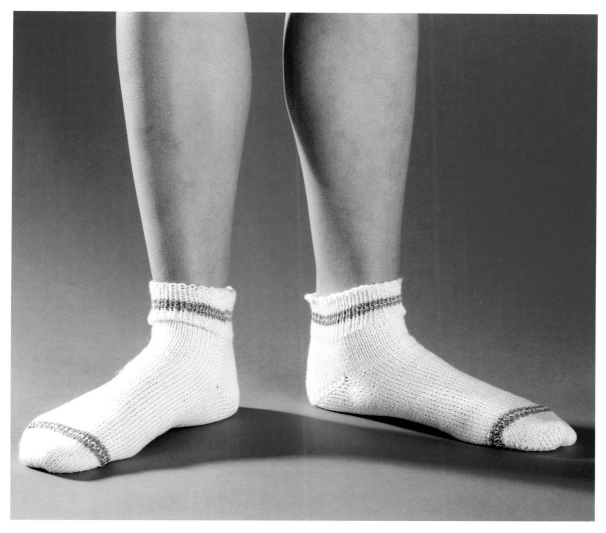

Toe

Worked in MC.

Follow short-row shaping as previously done for the heel.

Remove sts from loom as follows:

Place on dpn 1: Sts from pegs 1–32.

Place on dpn 2: Sts from pegs 33–64.

Sts are now prepared to graft close.

Follow grafting instructions to close the toe (see page 17 for illustrated instructions).

Finishing

Weave all yarn tail ends.

Block lightly.

Ropes

Cables and colorwork together at last. These are very special socks—you'll want to show them off!

LEVEL 4

MATERIALS

Knitting loom

64 peg extra fine gauge loom.

Yarn

350–400 yd (320–365 m) of sock weight yarn. (Sample uses Louet Gems 100% merino wool, 185 yd [169 m] per 1¾ oz [50 g].) 1 x skein in Teal 1 x skein in Gray

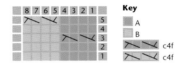

1 SUPER FINE

Tools

Knitting tool
Cable needle
Tapestry needle
2 double pointed needles size 2 (US)

Gauge

18 sts and 24 rows to 2 in. (5 cm) in St st (knit all rows)

Size

Shown in 8 in. (20.5 cm) foot circumference.

Abbreviations

A is Teal yarn.
B is Gray yarn.

Adapt

Can be adapted to any other loom with a peg multiple of 2.

Pattern note

Follow instructions on pages 20–21 for cables over 4 stitches.

Stitch pattern:
Rib stitch

Rnd 1: *k2, p2: rep from * to the end of rnd.
Repeat rnd 1.

Ropes stitch pattern

| | | | | | | | | | **Key** |
|8|7|6|5|4|3|2|1| | |

Key:
A
B
c4f
c4f

Rnd 1: (RS) k4 with A, k4 with B.
Rnd 2: k4 with A, k4 with B.
Rnd 3: Using A c4f, k4 with B.
Rnd 4: k4 with A, k4 with B.
Rnd 5: k4 with A, using B c4f.

Pinstripes pattern

Rnd 1: (RS) k1 with A, k1 with B.

Directions

With A, cast on 64 pegs, join to work in the round.

Cuff

With A, work ½ in. (1 cm) in rib stitch.

Set up for leg:
Next rnd: *k4 with A, k4 with B, rep from * to the end of rnd.

(The yarns are now positioned in the correct order to work the ropes chart.)

Leg

Rnds 1–5: Start and work the 2 color ropes cable pattern and repeat rnds 1–5 until leg measures 6 in. (15 cm) from cast-on edge. End on a row 5. Note: do not cut B.

Heel

Done completely in A in rows as in a flat panel using short-rows on 32 pegs. Follow short-row shaping instructions on page 25 until 12 sts remain unwrapped. End ready for a clockwise row. Continue with the reverse short-row shaping instructions on page 26. Cut A leaving a 6-in. (15-cm) tail. Continue with B.

Foot

Worked in the round. Sole and instep is worked in pinstripe pattern with both A and B colors until foot measures 6 ½ in. (16.5 cm) from back of heel. Cut B leaving a 6-in. (15-cm) tail.
Next rnd: Knit.

Toe

Done in A.
Follow short-row shaping as previously done for the heel.

Remove sts from loom as follows:
Place on dpn 1: Sts from pegs 1–32.
Place on dpn 2: Sts from pegs
33–64.

Sts are now prepared to graft close.
Follow grafting instructions to close
the toe (see page 17 for illustrated
instructions).

Finishing
Weave all yarn tail ends.
Block lightly.

PART IV

Fancy socks: cables & beads

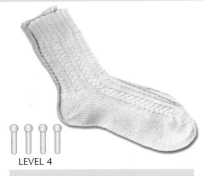

LEVEL 4

MATERIALS

Knitting loom

72 peg extra fine gauge knitting loom. (WonderSock loom was used in sample.)

Yarn

350–400 yd (320–365 m) of sock weight yarn. (Sample uses Louet Gems 100% merino wool, 185 yd [170 m] per 1¾ oz [50 g] in Cream.)

1 SUPER FINE

Tools

Knitting tool
Tapestry needle
2 double pointed needles size 2 (US)

Gauge

18 sts and 24 rows to 2 in. (5 cm) in St st (knit all rows)

Size

Shown as 9½ in. (24 cm) foot circumference.

Adapt

Can be adapted to any other (smaller or larger) loom with a peg multiple of 12.

Aran socks

My introduction to the fiber world came via my Grandma, my Abuelita—she was always knitting or crocheting. A recurrent motif in her designs was cables. I am fascinated by the beauty they add to a knitted fabric.

Stitch pattern:
Cable rib stitch

Read chart from bottom up. Every round is read from right to left. Work from chart or follow written directions.

Key
☐ Purl
☐ Knit
⧗ c4f
⧗ c4b

Rnd 1: *k2, p2: rep from * to end of rnd.
Rep rnd 1.

C4f

This is a left cross (LC)—4 stitch. Follow the step-by-step instructions on pages 20–21.

C4b

This is a right cross (RC)—4 stitch. Follow the step-by-step instructions on pages 20–21.

Cable rib stitch pattern

Rnd 1: (RS) k1, p2, k2, c4f, p2, k1.
Rnd 2: k1, p2, k6, p2, k1.
Rnd 3: k1, p2, c4b, k2, p2, k1.
Rnd 4: k1, p2, k6, p2, k1.
Repeat these 4 rows for pattern.

Directions

Cast on 72 sts, join to work in the round.

Cuff

Work in rib st for 2 in. (5 cm).

Leg

Start and work in cable rib stitch and repeat until leg measures 6½ in. (16.5 cm) from cast-on edge.

Heel

Done in rows as in a flat panel using short-rows on 36 pegs. Follow short-row shaping instructions on page 25 until 13 sts remain unwrapped. End ready for a clockwise row. Continue with the reverse short-row shaping instructions on page 26.

Foot

Worked in the round. Sole is worked in St st, upper section of foot continues in cable rib stitch.
Next rnd: k36, continue cable rib pattern on remaining pegs. Continue in St st and cable patt as set until foot measures 2 in. (5 cm) less than desired length (7½ in. [19 cm] for our sample).

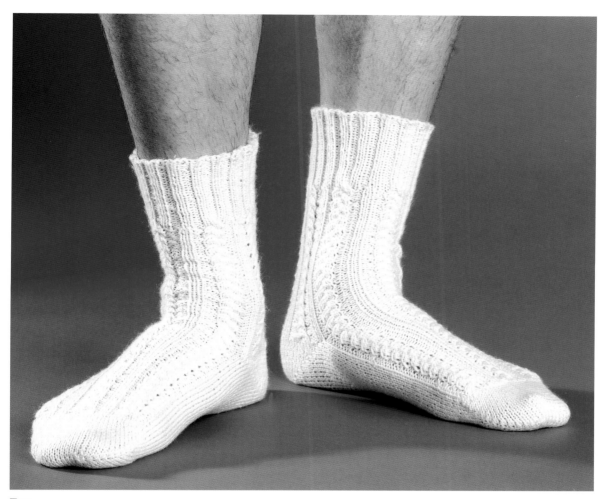

Toe

Follow short-row shaping as
previously done for the heel.
Remove sts from loom as follows:
Place on dpn 1: Sts from pegs 1–36.
Place on dpn 2: Sts from pegs
37–72.
Sts are now prepared to graft close.
Follow grafting instructions to close
the toe (see page 17 for illustrated
instructions).

Finishing

Weave all yarn tail ends.
Block lightly.

Braid cable socks

A small cable at each side of the socks give this pair of socks its defining feature. Choose a plain yarn for the cable to show the best.

LEVEL 3

MATERIALS

Knitting loom

64 peg extra fine gauge loom. (WonderSock loom was used in sample.)

Yarn

350–400 yards of sock weight yarn. (Sample uses Louet Gems 100% merino wool, 185 yd [170 m] per 1¾ oz [50 g] in Red Currant.)

1 SUPER FINE

Tools

Knitting tool
Cable needle
Tapestry needle
2 double pointed needles size 2 (US)

Gauge

18 sts and 21 rows to 2 in. (5 cm) in St st (knit all rows)

Size

Shown in 8½ in. (21.5 cm) foot circumference.

Adapt

To re-create the pattern, you will need to place the Braid Cable Chart on the first 10 sts of the loom.

Stitch patterns:

Rib stitch

Rnd 1: *k2, p2: rep from * to the end of rnd.
Repeat rnd 1.

Braided cable

C4f

This is a left cross (LC)—4 stitch. Follow the step-by-step instructions on pages 20–21.

C4b

This is a right cross (RC)—4 stitch. Follow the step-by-step instructions on pages 20–21.

Braid stitch pattern

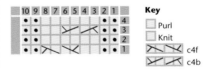

Row 1: p2, k2, c4f, p2.
Row 2: p2, k6, p2.
Row 3: p2, c4b, k2, p2.
Row 4: p2, k6, p2.

Directions

Cast on 64 sts, join to work in the round.

Right leg
Cuff

Work in rib stitch for 2 in. (5 cm).

Leg

Rnd 1–4: Place the braid cable stitch on the first 10 sts and follow the chart provided, knit to the end of rnd.

Repeat rnds 1–4 until leg measures 6 in. (15 cm) from cast-on edge (or desired length). End on a Row 3 of Braid cable chart.

Heel

Cut yarn and attach to peg 6. Peg 6 is peg 1 from this point forward. Done in rows as in a flat panel using short-rows on 32 pegs. Follow short-row shaping instructions on page 25 until 12 sts remain unwrapped. End ready for a clockwise row. Continue with the reverse short-row shaping instructions on page 26.

Toe

Follow short-row shaping as previously done for the heel. Remove sts from loom as follows: Place on dpn 1: Sts from pegs 32–1. Place on dpn 2: Sts from pegs 33–64.
Stitches are now prepared to graft close. Follow grafting instructions on page 17 to close the toe.

Finishing

Weave all yarn tail ends.
Block lightly.

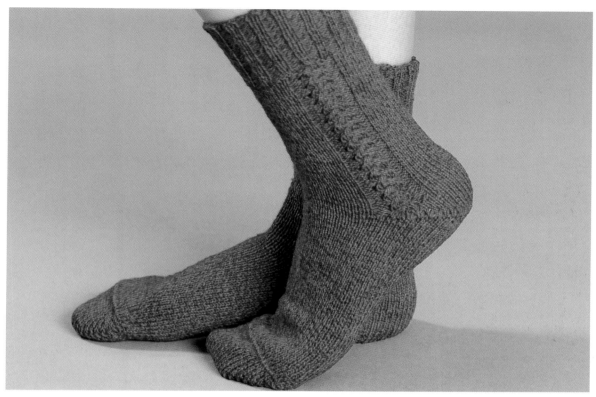

Left Leg

Cast on 64 sts, join to work in
the round.

Cuff

Work in rib stitch for 2 in. (5 cm).

Leg

Rnd 1–4: k32, place the Braid
cable stitch on next 10 sts (pegs 33
through 42) and follow the chart
provided, knit to the end of rnd.
Repeat rnds 1–4 until leg measures
6 in. (15 cm) from cast-on edge (or
desired length). End on a row 3 of
Braid cable chart.

Heel shaping, foot, and toe

Work as right leg.

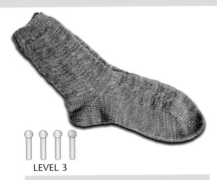

Twists and bricks

In a moment of indecision, this stitch pattern was born—with a little bit of basketweave, a few cables and twists thrown in and you have a whole new design.

LEVEL 3

MATERIALS

Knitting loom

64 peg extra fine gauge loom. (WonderSock loom was used in sample.)

Yarn

300–350 yd (274–320 m) of sock weight yarn. (Sample uses Malabrigo sock 100% superwash merino wool 440 yd [400 m] per 4 oz (100 g) in Lettuce.)

1 SUPER FINE

Tools

Knitting tool
Tapestry needle
2 double pointed needles size 2 (US)
Cable needle (cn)

Gauge

18 sts and 24 rows to 2 in. (5 cm) in St st (knit all rows).

Size

Shown in 8½ in. (21.5 cm) foot circumference.

Adapt

Can be adapted to any other (smaller or larger) loom with a peg multiple of 8.

Pattern note

Follow instructions on pages 20–21 for cables over 4 stitches.

Stitch pattern:
Twists & bricks

(multiple of 8 + 4)
Read chart from bottom up. Every round is read from right to left.

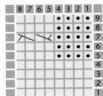

Key
• Purl
□ Knit
⤬ c4f

Rnds 1–4: k8.
Rnds 5 and 6: p4, k4.
Rnd 7: p4, c4f.
Rnds 8 and 9: p4, k4.

Directions

Cast on 64 sts, work in the round.

Cuff

Rnds 1–10: *k2, p2; rep from * to the end of rnd.

Leg

Rnds 1–9: Work twists & bricks stitch pattern.
Repeat last 9 rnds until leg measures 6 in. (15 cm) from cast-on edge or desired length. End on a row 4 of chart.

Heel

Cut yarn and attach to peg 63. Peg 63 is peg 1 from this point forward.

Done in rows as in a flat panel using short-rows on 32 pegs. Follow short-row shaping instructions on page 25 until 12 sts remain unwrapped. End ready for a clockwise row. Continue with the reverse short-row shaping instructions on page 26.

Foot

**Next rnd: k32, k2, p4, *k4, p4; rep from * to last 2sts, k2.
Next rnd: k32, k2, p4, *k4, p4; rep from * to last 2sts, k2.
Next rnd: k32, k2, p4, *c4f, p4; rep from * to last 2sts, k2.
Next rnd: k32, k2, p4, *k4, p4; rep from * to last 2sts, k2.
Next rnd: k32, k2, p4, *k4, p4; rep from * to last 2sts, k2.
Next 4 rnds: Knit to the end of rnd.**
Rep from ** to ** until foot measures desired length (7 in. [18 cm]) from back of heel.

Toe

Follow short-row shaping as previously done for the heel. Remove sts from loom as follows: Place on dpn 1: Sts from pegs 1–32. Place on dpn 2: Sts from pegs 33–64. The sts are now prepared to graft close. Follow grafting instructions to close the toe (see page 17 for illustrated instructions).

Finishing

Weave in all yarn tail ends. Block lightly.

Clustered cables

When you have a craving for cables, this cluster of cables will not disappoint. Grab your favorite yarn and get going!

LEVEL 3

MATERIALS

Knitting loom

64 peg extra fine gauge knitting loom. (WonderSock loom was used in sample.)

Yarn

350–400 yd (320–365 m) of sock weight yarn. (Sample uses Patons Kroy Heathers, 75% wool 25% Nylon, 152 yd [140 m] per 1¾ oz [50 g] in Gray.)

SUPER FINE 1

Tools

Knitting tool
Tapestry needle
2 double pointed needles size 2 (US)
Cable needle

Gauge

18 sts and 24 rows to 2 in. (5 cm) in St st (knit all rows)

Size

Shown in 8½ in. (21.5 cm) foot circumference.

Adapt

Can be adapted to any other (smaller or larger) loom with a peg multiple of 8.

Pattern note

Follow instructions on pages 20–21 for cables over 4 stitches.

Stitch pattern:
Clustered cable

Multiple of 8 + 4

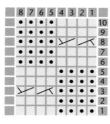

Key
● Purl
☐ Knit

⤰ c4b

Rnds 1–2: p4, k4.
Rnd 3: p4, c4f.
Rnds 4–5: p4, k4.
Rnds 6–7: k4, p4.
Rnd 8: C4f, p4.
Rnds 9–10: k4, p4.

Directions

Cast on 64 sts, join to work in the round.

Cuff

Rnd 1: *k2, p2; rep from * to the end of round
Repeat rnd 1 until cuff measures ½ in. (1.5 cm) from cast-on edge.

Leg

Start and work clustered cable pattern until leg measures 6 in. (15 cm) from cast-on edge.

Heel

Done in rows as in a flat panel using short-rows on 32 pegs. Follow short-row shaping instructions on page 25 until 12 sts remain unwrapped. End ready for a clockwise row. Continue with the reverse short-row shaping instructions on page 26.

Foot

Worked in the round. Foot is worked completely in St st (knit every round) until foot measures 6½ in. (16.5 cm) from back of heel (or desired length).

Toe

Follow short-row shaping as previously done for the heel. Remove sts from loom as follows:
Place on dpn 1: Sts from pegs 1–32.
Place on dpn 2: Sts from pegs 33–64. Sts are now prepared to graft close. Follow grafting instructions to close the toe (see page 17 for illustrated instructions).

Finishing

Weave all yarn tail ends. Block lightly.

Cascading socks

For those extra cold days, try these warmers—thick, strong, and deliciously comfortable.

LEVEL 3

MATERIALS

Knitting loom

64 peg extra fine gauge knitting loom. (WonderSock loom was used in sample.)

Yarn

350–400 yd (320–365 m) of sock weight yarn. (Sample uses Louet Gems 100% merino wool, 185 yd [169 m] per 1¾ oz [50 g] in Pink Panther.)

1 SUPER FINE

Tools

Knitting tool
Cable needle
Tapestry needle
2 double pointed needles size 2 (US)

Gauge

18 sts and 24 rows to 2 in. (5 cm) in St st (knit all rows)

Size

Shown in 8½ in. (21.5 cm) foot circumference.

Adapt

Can be adapted to any other (smaller or larger) loom with a peg multiple of 8.

Pattern note

Follow instructions on pages 20–21 for cables over 2 stitches.

Stitch pattern:
Right twist cable

8	7	6	5	4	3	2	1		Key
								4	● Purl
								3	▢ Knit
								2	⧫ Right twist (RFT)
								1	

Rnd 1: p2, k4, p2.
Rnd 2: p2 (right cross) 2 times, p2.
Rnd 3: p2, k4, p2.
Rnd 4: p2, k1, right cross, k1, p2.

Directions

Cast on 64 sts, work in the round.

Cuff

Rnds 1–10: *k2, p2: rep from * to the end of rnd.

Leg

Start and work in right twist cable pattern until sock measures 4 in. (10 cm) from cast-on edge, ending on a rnd 4.

Heel

Done in rows as in a flat panel using short-rows on 32 pegs. Follow short-row shaping instructions on page 25 until 12 sts remain unwrapped. Continue with the reverse short-row shaping instructions on page 26.

Foot

Worked in the round. Sole is worked in St st and instep is worked in pattern until foot measures desired length from back of heel (6½ in. [16.5 cm] for sample). Knit 1 additional row before beginning the toe.

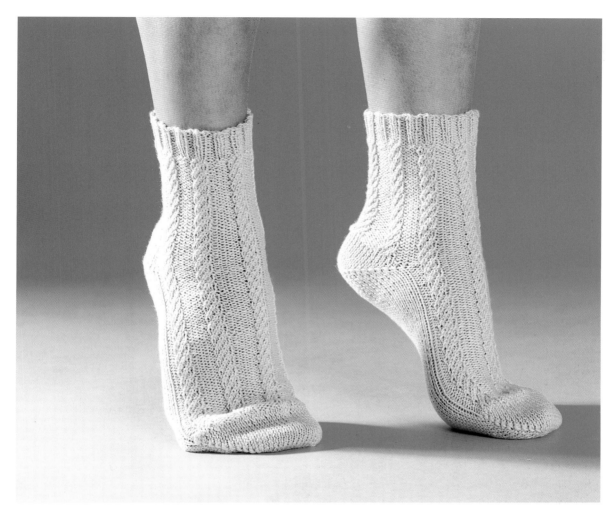

Toe

Follow short-row shaping as
previously done for the heel.
Remove sts from loom as follows:
Place on dpn 1: Sts from pegs 32–1.
Place on dpn 2: Sts from pegs
33–64.
Sts are now prepared to graft
closed. Follow grafting instructions
to close the toe (see pages 17 for
illustrated instructions).

Finishing

Weave in all yarn tail ends.
Block lightly.

Snaking socks

This pattern explores cables over 2 stitches which snake over the foot of the sock.

LEVEL 3

MATERIALS

Knitting loom

64 peg extra fine gauge loom. (WonderSock loom was used in sample.)

Yarn

350–400 yd (320–365 m) of sock weight yarn. (Sample uses Malabrigo sock 100% superwash merino wool 440 yd [400 m] per 4 oz [100 g] in Violeta Africana.)

1 SUPER FINE

Tools

Knitting tool
2 double pointed needles
size 2 (US)
Tapestry needle
Cable needle

Gauge

18 sts and 24 rows to 2 in. (5 cm) in St st (knit all rows)

Size

Shown in 8½ in. (21.5 cm) foot circumference.

Adapt

Can be adapted to any other (smaller or larger) loom with a peg multiple of 4.

Pattern note

Follow instructions on pages 20–21 for cables over 2 stitches.

Stitch pattern:
Twist stitch

Work from chart.
Read chart from bottom up. Every round is read from right to left.

Key
• Purl
☐ Knit
⋋⋌ Left twist (LFT)
⋎⋌ Right twist (RFT)

Cuff

Rnd 1: *p1, k2, p1: rep from * to the end of round.
Repeat rnd 1.

Leg

Start and work in twist stitch pattern until leg measures 6½ in. (16.5 cm) from cast-on edge. Be sure to end on a rnd 4 from pattern.

Heel

Done in rows as in a flat panel using short-rows on 32 pegs. Follow short-row shaping instructions on page 25 until 12 sts remain unwrapped. End ready for a clockwise row. Continue with the reverse short-row shaping instructions on page 26.

Foot

Worked in the round.

Next rnd: k32, follow twist pattern to the end of the round.
Continue in patt and st st as set by last rnd until foot measures 6½ in. (16.5 cm) from back of heel (or desired length). End on a rnd 1 or rnd 3 of chart.

Toe

Follow short-row shaping as for the heel.

Remove sts from loom as follows:

Place on dpn 1: Sts from pegs 32–1.

Place on dpn 2: Sts from pegs 33–64.

Sts are now prepared to graft close. Follow grafting instructions to close the toe (see page 17 for illustrated instructions).

Finishing

Weave all yarn tail ends.

Block lightly.

Trellis

The trellis stitch pattern looks great but is a bit of a challenge as it combines right twists, left twists, and purled twists. The stitch pattern was inspired by gothic windows.

LEVEL 4

MATERIALS

Knitting loom

64 peg extra fine gauge loom. (WonderSock loom was used in sample.)

Yarn

350–400 yd (320–365 m) of sock weight yarn. (Sample uses Malabrigo sock 100% superwash merino wool 440 yd [400 m] per 4 oz [100 g] in Impressionist Sky.)

1 SUPER FINE

Tools

Knitting tool
Tapestry needle
2 double pointed needles size 2 US)
Cable needle

Gauge

18 sts and 22 rows to 2 in. (5 cm) in St st (knit all rows)

Size

Shown in 8½ in. (21.5 cm) foot circumference.

Adapt

Can be adapted to any other (smaller or larger) loom with a peg multiple of 8.

Pattern note

Knit stitch can be substituted for flat stitch. Follow instructions on pages 20–21 for cables and purled cables over 2 stitches.

Stitch pattern:

Rib stitch

Rnd 1: *k2, p2; rep from * to the end of rnd.
Rep rnd 1.

Trellis stitch pattern

Read chart from bottom up. Every round is read from right to left.

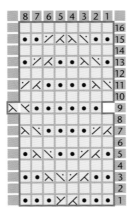

Key

- **Purl** — Purl stitch
- **Knit** — Knit stitch
- **Right twist** — st1 to CN, hold to back, k1 from 2nd peg and place on 1st peg, k1 from CN, place on 2nd peg.
- **Left twist** — st1 to CN, hold in front, k1 from 2nd peg and place on 1st peg, k1 from CN, place on 2nd peg.
- **Right twist, purl bg** — st1 to CN, hold in back, k1 and place on peg 1, p1 from CN and place on peg 2.
- **Left twist purl, bg** — st1 to CN, hold in front, p1 and place on peg 1, k1 from CN and place on peg 2.

Right twist purl bg

1. Take stitch from peg 1 to cable needle, hold in back.
2. K1 and place on peg 1, p1 from cable needle and place on peg 2.

Left twist purl bg

1. Take stitch from peg 1 to cable needle, hold in front.
2. P1, place on peg 1, k1 from cable needle and place on peg.

Directions

Cast on 64 sts, join to work in the round.

Cuff

Work in rib pattern for 2 in. (5 cm).

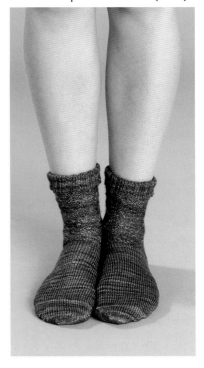

Leg
Rnds 1–16: Work trellis chart (the chart repeats 8 times on a round). Repeat rnds 1–16 until leg measures 6 in. (15 cm) from cast-on edge (or desired length). End on a row 16.

Heel
Done in rows as in a flat panel using short-rows on 32 pegs. Follow short-row shaping instructions on page 25 until 12 sts remain unwrapped. End ready for a clockwise row. Continue with the reverse short-row shaping instructions on page 26.

Foot
Worked in the round. Sole and instep are worked in St st (knit every round) until foot measures 7 in. (18 cm) from back of heel (or desired length).

Toe
Follow short-row shaping as previously done for the heel. Remove sts from loom as follows: Place on dpn 1: Sts from pegs 1–32. Place on dpn 2: Sts from pegs 33–64. Sts are now prepared to graft close. Follow grafting instructions to close the toe (see page 17 for illustrated instructions).

Finishing
Weave all yarn tail ends. Block lightly.

Hourglass socks

These socks are similar to the Trellis socks with the exception that the cables do not cross at the end of the traveling stitches.

LEVEL 4

MATERIALS

Knitting loom

64 peg extra fine gauge loom. (WonderSock loom was used in sample.)

Yarn

350–400 yd (320–365 m) of fingering weight yarn. (Sample used Berroco Comfort Sock, 50% Super Fine Nylon 50% Super Fine Acrylic 447 yd [412 m] per 3½ oz [100 g] in Gray.)

1 SUPER FINE

Tools

Knitting tool
Cable needle
Tapestry needle

Gauge

16 sts and 23 rows to 2 in. (5 cm) in St st (knit all rows)

Adapt

Can be adapted to any other (smaller or larger) loom with a peg multiple of 8.

Stitch pattern:
Hourglass

Read chart from bottom up. Every round is read from right to left. Work from chart or use following instructions. See pages 20–21 for right cross purl and left cross purl.

Key

- • Purl
- ☐ Knit
- LCP
- RCP

Rnd 1: p3, k2, p3.
Rnd 2: p3, k2, p3.
Rnd 3: p2, RCP, LCP, p2.
Rnd 4: p2, k1, p2, k1, p2.
Rnd 5: p1, RCP, p2, LCP, p1.
Rnd 6: p1, k1, p4, k1, p1.
Rnd 7: RCP, p4, LCP.
Rnd 8: k1, p6, k1.
Rnd 9: k1, p6, k1.
Rnd 10: k1, p6, k1.
Rnd 11: LCP, p4, RCP.
Rnd 12: p1, k1, p4, k1, p1.
Rnd 13: p1, LCP, p2, RCP, p1.
Rnd 14: p2, k1, p2, k1, p2.

Rnd 15: p2, LCP, RCP, p2.
Rnd 16: p3, k2, p3.

Directions

Cast on 64 sts, join to work in the round.

Cuff

Rnd 1: *K1, p2, k1; rep from * to the end of rnd.
Rep rnd 1, 12 more times.

Leg

Rnds 1–16: Work hourglass stitch pattern.
Repeat last 16 rnds until leg measures 7 in. (18 cm) from cast-on edge. End on a round 15.

Heel

Done in rows as in a flat panel using short-rows on 32 pegs. Follow short-row shaping instructions on page 25 until 12 sts remain unwrapped. End ready for a clockwise row. Continue with the reverse short-row shaping instructions on page 26.

Foot

Next rnd: k32, *p3, k2, p3; rep from * to the end of rnd.
Next 16 rnds: k32, work hourglass pattern on next 32 sts. Repeat last 16 rnds until foot measures 7 in. (18 cm) from back of heel (or desired length). End on any of these rows 1, 2, 8, 9, 10, or 16.

Toe

Follow short-row shaping as previously done for heel.
Remove sts from loom as follows:
Place on dpn 1: Sts from pegs 1–32.
Place on dpn 2: Sts from pegs 33–64.
Sts are now prepared to graft close.
Follow grafting instructions to close the toe (see page 17 for illustrated instructions).

Finishing

Weave all yarn tail ends.
Block lightly.

Starry night socks

These starry night socks have beads positioned at different intervals on the cuff. Change the bead colors and see the entire design change.

LEVEL 3

MATERIALS

Knitting loom

64 peg extra fine gauge loom. (WonderSock loom was used here.)

Yarn

350–400 yd (320–365 m) of sock weight yarn. (Sample uses Louet Gems 100% merino wool, 185 yd [170 m] per 1¾ oz [50 g] in Black.)

1 SUPER FINE

Tools

Knitting tool
Tapestry needle
2 double pointed needles size 2 (US)

Other

256 beads size 6 in color of choice (light blue was used in sample).

Gauge

18 sts and 24 rows to 2 in. (5 cm) in St st (knit all rows)

Size

Shown in 8½ in. (21.5 cm) foot circumference.

Adapt

Can be adapted to any other (smaller or larger) loom with a peg multiple of 8.

Pattern note

Thread 128 beads onto the yarn before starting the sock. See page 22 for tips with working with beads.

Stitch patterns:
Little Stars
Rnd 1: k2, slbd, k5.
Rnd 2: k8.
Rnd 3: k6, slbd, k1.

Key
☐ Knit
✴ Bead

Rib stitch

Rnd 1: *k2, p2: rep from * to the end of rnd.
Repeat rnd 1.

Directions

Cast on 64 sts, join to work in the round.

Cuff

Work 2 in. (5 cm) in rib pattern.

Leg

Next 2 rnds: Knit.
Next 3 rnds: Work Little Stars chart (above).
Repeat chart pattern until leg measures 4 in. (10 cm) from cast-on edge.
Next 5 rnds: Knit.

Heel

Done in rows as in a flat panel using short-rows on 32 pegs. Follow short-row shaping instructions on page 25 until 12 sts remain unwrapped. End ready for a clockwise row. Continue with the reverse short-row shaping instructions on page 26.

Foot

Worked in the round in St st until foot measures 7 in. (18 cm) from back of heel (or desired length).

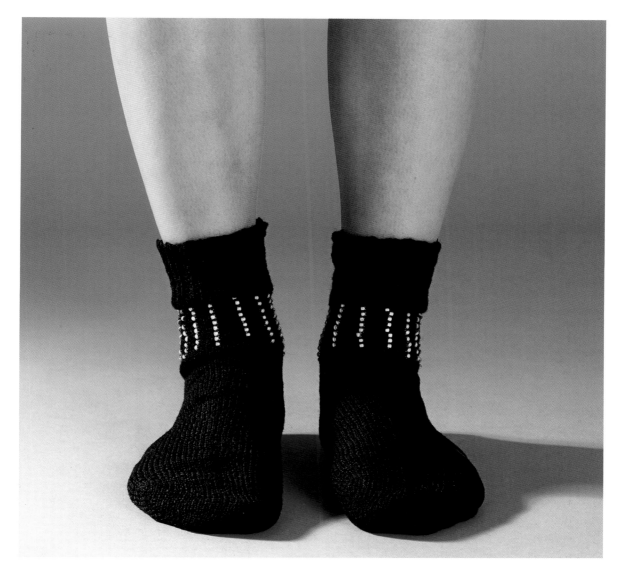

Toe

Follow short-row shaping as
previously done for the heel.
Remove sts from loom as follows:
Place on dpn 1: Sts from pegs 1–32.
Place on dpn 2: Sts from pegs
33–64.
Sts are now prepared to graft close.
Follow grafting instructions to close
the toe (see page 17 for illustrated
instruction).

Finishing

Weave all yarn tail ends.
Block lightly.

Beaded peaks

This sparkly design is perfect for a completely unique pair of socks. You could also use beads of a contrasting color for a more playful style.

LEVEL 3

MATERIALS

Knitting loom

64 peg extra fine gauge loom. (WonderSock loom was used here.)

Yarn

350–400 yd (320–365 m) of sock weight yarn. (Sample uses Malabrigo sock 100% superwash merino wool 440 yd [402 m] per 4 oz [100 g] in Impressionist Sky.)

1 SUPER FINE

Tools

Knitting tool
Tapestry needle
2 double pointed needles size 2 (US)

Other

512 beads size 6 in color of choice (blue was used in sample).

Gauge

18 sts and 24 rows to 2 in. (5 cm) in St st (knit all rows).

Size

Shown in 8½ in. (21.5 cm) foot circumference.

Adapt

Can be adapted to any other (smaller or larger) loom with a peg multiple of 8.

Stitch patterns:

Rib stitch

Rnd 1: *k2, p2; rep from * to the end of rnd.
Repeat rnd 1.

Bead peaks

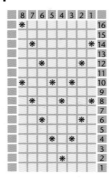

Key

☐ 1 st and 1 row
✳ slbd

Rnd 1 and alternate rows: k8.
Rnd 2: k3, slbd, k4.
Rnd 4: k2, slbd, k1, slbd, k3.
Rnd 6: k1, slbd, k3, slbd, k2.
Rnd 8: slbd, k2, slbd, k2, slbd, k1.
Rnd 10: k2, slbd, k1, slbd, k2, slbd.
Rnd 12: k1, slbd, k3, slbd, k2.
Rnd 14: slbd, k5, slbd, k1.
Rnd 16: k7, slbd.

Directions

See page 22 for tips with working with beads.

Cuff

Work in rib pattern for 2 in. (5 cm).

Leg

Next rnd: Work 3 rows of St st.
Next 32 rnds: Work 2 repetitions of bead peaks pattern.
Next rnd: Continue working in St st until leg measures 6½ in. (16.5 cm) from cast-on edge.

Heel

Done in rows as in a flat panel using short-rows on 32 pegs. Follow short-row shaping instructions on page 25 until 12 sts remain unwrapped. End ready for a clockwise row. Continue with the reverse short-row shaping instructions on page 26.

Foot

Worked in the round. Sole and foot are worked in St st. Continue working in St st until foot measures desired length from back of heel (7 in. [18 cm] for our sample).

Toe

Follow short-row shaping as previously done for the heel. Remove sts from loom as follows: Place on dpn 1: Sts from pegs 32–1. Place on dpn 2: Sts from pegs 33–64.
Sts are now prepared to graft close. Follow grafting instructions to close the toe (see page 17 for illustrated instructions).

Finishing

Weave all yarn tail ends.
Block lightly.

Waves

The cable moves around the sock in a wave-like fashion, creating a wonderfully textured effect.

LEVEL 3

MATERIALS

Knitting loom

60 peg extra fine gauge knitting loom. (WonderSock loom was used in sample.)

Yarn

300–350 yd (274–320 m) of sock weight yarn. (Sample uses Malabrigo sock 100% superwash merino wool, 440 yd [402 m] per 4 oz [100 g] in Stonechat.)

1 SUPER FINE

Tools

Knitting tool
Tapestry needle
Cable needle
2 double pointed needles size 2 (US)

Gauge

18 sts and 22 rows to 2 in. (5 cm) in St st (knit all rows)

Size

Shown in 8½ in. (21.5 cm) foot circumference.

Adapt

Can be adapted to any other (smaller or larger) loom with a peg multiple of 6.

Stitch pattern:
Waves stitch

(Multiple of 6)
Follow instructions on pages 20–21 for cables over 4 stitches.

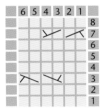

Key
☐ Knit
c4f
c4b

Rnds 1–2: k6.
Rnd 3: k2, c4f.
Rnds 4–6: k6.
Rnd 7: c4b, k2.
Rnd 8: k6.

Directions

Cast on 60 sts, join to work in the round.

Cuff

Rnd 1–10: *k1, p1; rep from * to the end of round.

Leg

Rnds 1–8: Work waves pattern to the end of round.
Repeat last 8 rnds until leg measures 6 in. (15 cm) from cast-on edge.

Heel

Done in rows as in a flat panel using short-rows on 30 pegs. Follow short-row shaping instructions on page 25 until 12 sts remain unwrapped. End ready for a

clockwise row. Continue with the reverse short-row shaping instructions on page 26.

Foot

From this point forward, continue working in the round.
Work in St st until foot measures desired length (7 in. [18 cm]) from back of heel.

Toe

Follow short-row shaping as previously done for the heel.
Remove sts from loom as follows:
Place on dpn 1: Sts from pegs 1–32.
Place on dpn 2: Sts from pegs 33–64.
Sts are now prepared to graft close. Follow grafting instructions to close the toe (see page 17 for illustrated instructions).

Finishing

Weave all yarn tail ends.
Block lightly.

PART V
Lace socks

Ladder lace

This intermediate level pattern looks so effective with this Snapdragon yarn.

LEVEL 3

MATERIALS

Knitting loom

64 peg extra fine gauge loom. (WonderSock loom was used in sample.)

Yarn

350–400 yd (320–365 m) of sock weight yarn. (Sample uses Sweet Georgia Superwash Sock yarn, 100% superwash merino, 400 yd [365 m] per 3½ oz [100 g] in Snapdragon.)

1 SUPER FINE

Tools

Knitting tool
Tapestry needle
2 double pointed needles size 2 (US)

Gauge

18 sts and 21 rows to 2 in. (5 cm) in St st (knit all rows)

Size

Shown in size 8½ in. (21.5 cm) circumference.

Adapt

Can be adapted to any other (smaller or larger) loom with a peg multiple of 4.

Stitch patterns:

2x2 rib stitch

Rnd 1: *k2, p2; rep from * to the end of rnd.
Rep rnd 1.

Ladder lace

Read chart from bottom up. Every round is read from right to left. Work from chart or follow written directions.

Key
● Purl
☐ Knit
O yo
╱ k2tog
╲ ssk

Rnd 1: ssk, yo 2 times, k2tog.
Rnd 2: k*1, p1, k2.

Directions

Cast on 64 sts, join to work in the round.

Cuff

Work in 2x2 rib pattern until cuff measures 1½ in. (4 cm) from cast-on edge.

Leg

Rnds 1–2: Work ladder lace pattern to the end of rnd.
Repeat leg rnds 1 and 2 until leg measures 6 in. (15 cm) or desired leg length from cast-on edge. End on a row 2.

Heel

Done in rows as in a flat panel using short-rows on 32 pegs. Follow short-row shaping instructions on page 25 until 12 sts remain unwrapped. End ready for a clockwise row. Continue with the reverse short-row shaping instructions on page 26.

Foot

Worked in the round. Sole is worked in St st on first 32 sts, remaining 32sts make up the upper section of foot and continue in ladder lace pattern.
Next 2 rnds: K32, continue with ladder lace pattern.

Repeat last 2 rnds until foot measures 7 in. (18 cm) from back of heel (or desired length).

Toe

Follow short-row shaping as previously done for the heel. Remove sts from loom as follows: Place on dpn 1: Sts from pegs 1–32. Place on dpn 2: Sts from pegs 33–64. Sts are now prepared to graft close. Follow grafting instructions to close the toe (see page 17 for illustrated instructions).

Finishing

Weave all yarn tail ends. Block lightly.

Garden

Although tricky, this is a great project to try as the outcome is beautiful—detailed, soft, strong, and so comfortable!

LEVEL 4

MATERIALS

Knitting loom

64 peg extra fine gauge loom. (WonderSock loom was used in sample.)

Yarn

350–400 yd (320–365 m) of fingering weight yarn. (Sample uses Malabrigo sock 100% superwash merino wool 440 yd [400 m] per 3½ oz [100 g] in Lettuce.)

1 SUPER FINE

Tools

2 double pointed needles size 2 (US)
Tapestry needle

Gauge

16 sts and 21 rows to 2 in. (5 cm) in St st (knit all rows)

Size

Fits up to 9 in. (23 cm) leg circumference.

Adapt

Can be adapted to any other (smaller or larger) loom with a peg multiple of 8.

Stitch pattern:
Floral mesh

Read chart from bottom up. Every round is read from right to left. Multiple of 8 sts over 12 rounds. Work from chart or use following instructions.

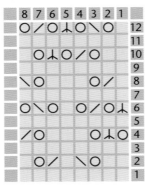

Key

- ☐ Knit
- ◯ yo
- ⋏ central dble dec
- ╱ k2tog
- ╲ ssk

Rnd 1: k8.
Rnd 2: k2, yo, ssk, k1, k2tog, yo, k1.
Rnd 3: k8.
Rnd 4: yo, dbl dec, yo, k3, yo, k2tog.
Rnd 5: k8.
Rnd 6: dble dec, yo, k2tog, yo, k1, yo, ssk, yo.
Rnd 7: k8.
Rnd 8: k1, k2tog, yo, k3, yo, ssk.
Rnd 9: k8.
Rnd 10: k2, yo, k2tog, yo, dbl dec, yo, k1.
Rnd 11: k8.

Rnd 12: k1, yo, ssk, yo, dbl dec, yo, k2tog, yo.

Directions

Cast on 64 sts, join to work in the round.

Cuff

Rnd 1: *k2, p2; repeat from * to the end of the round.
Repeat rnd 1 until cuff measures 1 in. (2.5 cm) from cast-on edge.

Leg

Rounds 1–12: Work floral mesh pattern (the pattern will repeat 8 times around the loom).
Repeat rnds 1–12 of pattern, 6 more times, or until desired leg length is achieved. Repeat row 1 of pattern.

Heel shaping

Done in rows as in a flat panel using short-rows on 32 pegs. Follow short-row shaping instructions on page 25 until 12 sts remain unwrapped. End ready for a clockwise row. Continue with the reverse short-row shaping instructions on page 26.

Next round: k32, maintain the floral mesh on the remaining 32 sts, until the foot measures 2 in. (5 cm) less from back of heel than desired length (7 in. [18 cm] for our sample).

Toe

Follow short-row shaping as previously done for the heel. Remove sts from loom as follows: Place on dpn 1: Sts from pegs 1–32. Place on dpn 2: Sts from pegs 33–64.

The sts are now prepared to graft close. Follow grafting instructions to close the toe (see page 17 for illustrated instructions).

Finishing

Weave all yarn tail ends. Block lightly.

Marbled socks

This particular yarn, together with the arrow lace pattern, creates a great marbled effect.

LEVEL 4

MATERIALS

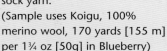

Knitting loom

70 peg extra fine gauge loom. (WonderSock loom was used in sample.)

Yarn

350–400 yd (320–365 m) of fingering weight sock yarn. (Sample uses Koigu, 100% merino wool, 170 yards [155 m] per 1¾ oz [50g] in Blueberry)

1 SUPER FINE

Tools

2 double pointed needles size 2 (US)
Tapestry needle

Gauge

16 sts and 21 rows to 2 in. (5 cm) in St st (knit all rows).

Size

9½ in. (24 cm) circumference.

Adapt

Can be adapted to any other (smaller or larger) loom with a peg multiple of 7.

Stitch pattern:
Arrow Lace Pattern

(7 st pattern repeat)
Rnd 1: k1, k2tog, yo, k1, yo, ssk, k1; rep across.
Rnd 2 and 4: Knit.
Rnd 4: k2tog, yo, k3, yo, ssk; rep across.

Directions

Cast on 70 sts and join to work in the round.

Picot edge cuff

Rnd 1–8: Knit.
Rnd 9: *k2tog, yo; rep from * to the end of rnd.
Rnd 10–18: Knit.
Bring up cast-on row for a cuff (see page 15).
Next rnd: Knit.

Leg

Rnds 1–4: Work in arrow lace pattern to the end of round.
Rep rnds 1–4 of leg 20 times or until leg reaches desired length.

Heel

Done in rows as in a flat panel using short-rows on 36 pegs. Follow short-row shaping instructions on page 25 until 13 sts remain unwrapped. End ready for a clockwise row. Continue with the reverse short-row shaping instructions on page 26.

Foot

Next rnd: Knit 35 sts, follow row 1–4 of arrow lace pattern on next 35 sts.
Continue in St st and lace pattern as set until foot measures 2 in. (5 cm) less than desired length.

Toe

In St st, follow short-row shaping as previously done for the heel.
Remove sts from loom as follows:
Place on dpn 1: Sts from pegs 35–1.
Place on don 2: Sts from pegs 36–70.
Sts are now prepared to graft close.
Follow grafting instructions to close the toe (see page 17 for illustrated instructions).

Finishing

Weave all yarn tail ends. Block lightly.

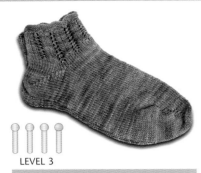

LEVEL 3

Little wisps of wheat

Sometimes all you need is a little bit of lace to make the pair of socks irresistible. Little wisps of wheat has a simple eyelet stitch pattern that provides a scalloped edge. Blocking the socks will allow the scalloped edge to show the most.

MATERIALS

Knitting loom

64 peg extra fine gauge knitting loom. (WonderSock loom was used in sample.)

Yarn

350–400 yd (320–365 m) of sock weight yarn. (Sample uses Malabrigo sock 100% superwash merino wool 440 yd [400 m] per 3½ oz [100 g] in Lettuce).

1 SUPER FINE

Tools

Knitting tool
Tapestry needle
2 double pointed needles size 2 (US)

Gauge

18 sts and 24 rows to 2 in. (5 cm) in St st (knit all rows).

Size

Shown in 8½ in (21.5 cm) foot circumference.

Adapt

Can be adapted to any other (smaller or larger) loom with a peg multiple of 8.

Stitch pattern:
Wheat pattern

(8 st repeat)
Read chart from bottom up. Every round is read from right to left.

Key
- Purl
- Knit
- ○ yo
- ╱ k2tog
- ╲ ssk

Rnd 1: k8.
Rnd 2: p1, yo, k1, ssk, k1, k2tog, k1.

Directions

Cast on 64 sts, join to work in the round.

Cuff & Leg

Rnd 1: Purl.
Rnd 2: Knit.
Rnd 3: Purl.
Rnd 4: Knit.
Next 2 rnds: Work wheat chart.
Repeat last 2 rnds 8 more times.
Next 5 rnds: Knit.

Heel

Done in rows as in a flat panel using short-rows on 32 pegs. Follow short-row shaping instructions on page 25 until 12 sts remain unwrapped. End ready for a clockwise row. Continue with the reverse short-row shaping instructions on page 26.

Foot

From this point forward, continue working in the round.
Work in St st until foot measures desired length (7 in. [18 cm]) from back of heel.

Toe

Follow short-row shaping as
previously done for the heel.
Remove sts from loom as follows:
Place on dpn 1: Sts from pegs 1–32.
Place on dpn 2: Sts from pegs
33–64.
Sts are now prepared to graft close.
Follow grafting instructions to close
the toe (see page 17 for illustrated
instructions).

Finishing

Weave all yarn tail ends.
Block lightly.

LEVEL 4

MATERIALS

Knitting loom

64 peg extra fine gauge loom. (WonderSock loom was used in sample.)

Yarn

300–350 yd (274–320 m) of sock weight yarn. (Sample uses Sweet Georgia superwash sock yarn, 100% superwash merino, 400 yd [365 m] per 3½ oz [100 g] in River.)

1 SUPER FINE

Tools

Knitting tool
Tapestry needle
2 double pointed needles size 2 (US)

Gauge

18 sts and 21 rows to 2 in. (5 cm) in St st (knit all rows).

Size

Shown in 8½ in. (21.5 cm) foot circumference.

Adapt

Can be adapted to any other (smaller or larger) loom with a peg multiple of 8.

Lazaro shells

I lived the first years of my life near the beach of Lazaro Cardenas. The stitch pattern and yarn used in these socks remind me of my childhood there. The blue represents the ocean, and the white and stitch pattern all the little shells.

Tip

Move the sts for the k2tog and ssk first, then knit the row as instructed.

Stitch pattern:
Little shells

(In multiple of 8 sts)
Read chart from bottom up. Every round is read from right to left. Work from chart or follow written directions.

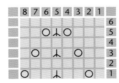

Key

☐ Knit
O yo
⅄ dble dec

Rnd 1: K1, yo, k2, dbl dec, k2, yo.
Rnd 2: K8.
Rnd 3: K2, yo, k1 dbl dec, k1, yo.
Rnd 4: K8.
Rnd 5: K3, yo, dbl dec, yo, k2.
Rnd 6: K8.

Directions

Cast on 64 sts, join to work in the round.

Cuff

Rnd 1–10: *k2, p2; rep from * to the end of round.

Leg

Rnds 1–6: Work little shell pattern to the end of round.
Repeat last 6 rnds until leg measures 6 in. (15 cm), or desired length, from cast-on edge.

Heel

Done in rows as in a flat panel using short-rows on 32 pegs. Follow short-row shaping instructions on page 25 until 12 sts remain unwrapped. End ready for a clockwise row. Continue with the reverse short-row shaping instructions on page 26.

Foot

From this point forward, continue working in the round.
Next 6 rnds: K32, continue little shell pattern on next 32sts. Repeat last 6 rnds until foot measures desired length (6½ in. [16.5 cm]) from back of heel.

Toe

Follow short-row shaping as previously done for the heel. Remove sts from loom as follows: Place on dpn 1: Sts from pegs 1–32. Place on dpn 2: Sts from pegs 33–64.
Sts are now prepared to graft close. Follow grafting instructions to close the toe (see page 17 for illustrated instructions).

Finishing

Weave all yarn tail ends.
Block lightly.

PART VI
Footsies & others

Cherlooms pedi socks

Pretty toes deserve to be shown. These pedi socks are perfect when wearing sandals or for the days when you are heading to the salon to get a pedicure. Keep your feet warm while still showing off your latest pedicure.

LEVEL 3

MATERIALS

Knitting loom

64 peg extra fine gauge loom. (WonderSock loom was used in sample).

Yarn

350–400 yd (320–365 m) of sock weight yarn. (Sample uses Koigu 100% merino wool, 175 yd [160 m] per 1¾ oz [50 g] in P407 91.)

1 SUPER FINE

Tools

Knitting tool
Cable needle
Tapestry needle

Gauge

18 st and 24 rows to 2 in. (5 cm) in St st (knit all rows).

Size

Shown in 8½ in. (21.5 cm) foot circumference.

Adapt

Can be adapted to any other (smaller or larger) loom with a peg multiple of 4.

Stitch pattern:
Rib stitch

Rnd 1: *p2, k2: rep from * to the end of round.
Repeat rnd 1.

Left twist stitch

Read chart from bottom up. Every round is read from right to left. Work from chart or follow written directions.

Key
- ● Purl
- ☐ Knit
- ╳ Left twist (LFT)

Rnd 1: p1, k2, p1.
Rnd 2: p1, LTW, p1.
Repeat these 2 rows for pattern.

Directions

Cuff
Work 1½ in. (4 cm) in rib pattern.

Leg
Rnd 1–2: Begin left twist pattern. Repeat pattern until leg measures 6 in. (15 cm), or desired length, from cast-on edge. Be sure to end on a rnd 2 of twist pattern.

Heel
Done in rows as in a flat panel using short-rows on 32 pegs. Follow short row shaping instructions on page 25 until 12 sts remain unwrapped. End ready for a clockwise row.

Continue with the reverse short row shaping instructions on page 26.

Foot
Worked in the round. Sole is worked in st st, upper section of foot continues in the left twist pattern.
Next 2 rnds: k32, repeat left twist pattern to end of round.
Repeat last 2 rounds until item measures 2½ in (6.5 cm) less than desired foot length (measure from back of heel). **

Work in rib pattern for ½ in.
(1.5 cm).

Bind off
Use basic bind-off (see page 16) to
remove loosely.

Finishing
Weave all yarn tail ends.
Block lightly.

Cherlooms Full Sock Option

Follow the instructions provided
for pedi sock to **.
Work 5 rounds in St st (knit
all sts).

Toe
Follow short-row shaping as
previously done for the heel.
Remove st from loom as follows:
Place on dpn 1: Sts from pegs
1–32.
Place on dpn 2: Sts from pegs
33–64.
Sts are now prepared to graft
close. Follow grafting instructions
to close the toe (see page 17 for
illustrated instructions).

Finishing
Weave all yarn tail ends.
Block lightly.

Pedi socks

These brighter versions are shorter on the ankles and are perfect for brightening up a spring outfit.

LEVEL 2

MATERIALS

Knitting loom

64 peg extra fine gauge knitting loom. (WonderSock loom was used in sample.)

Yarn

350–400 yd (320–365 m) of sock weight yarn. (Sample uses Sweet Georgia Boheme 100% superwash merino, 185 yd [165 m] per 1¾ oz [50 g] in Hard Candy.)

Tools

Knitting tool

Gauge

18 sts and 24 rows to 2 in. (5 cm) in St st (knit all rows).

Size

Shown in 8½ in. (21.5 cm) foot circumference.

Adapt

Can be adapted to any other (smaller or larger) loom with a peg multiple of 4.

Pattern stitch:
Rib stitch

Rnd 1: *k2, p2: rep from * to the end of round.
Repeat rnd 1.

Directions

Cast on 64 sts, join to work in the round.

Cuff

Work 1 in. (2.5 cm) in rib stitch.

Leg

Rnd 1: Knit.
Rep rnd 1 until leg measures 2 in. (5 cm) from cast-on edge.

Heel

Done in rows as in a flat panel using short-rows on 32 pegs. Follow short-row shaping instructions on page 25 until 12 sts remain unwrapped. End ready for a clockwise row. Continue with the reverse short-row shaping instructions on page 26.

Foot

Worked in the round. Sole and instep are worked in St st until foot measures desired length (5½ in. [14 cm] for our sample). Work in rib pattern for ½ in. (1.5 cm).

Bind off

Use basic bind-off (see page 16 for illustrated instructions) to remove loosely.

Finishing

Weave all yarn tail ends. Block lightly.

Early dawn yoga socks

Perfect for yoga or dance as your toes and heels can grip.
Optional heel instructions are provided.

LEVEL 2

MATERIALS

Knitting loom

64 peg extra fine gauge loom.
(WonderSock loom was used in
sample.)

Yarn

350–400 yd (320–365 m)
of sock weight yarn.
(Sample uses Cascade
Yarn, 100% Peruvian highland,
220 yd [200 m] per 3½ oz [100
g] in # 9825.)

1 SUPER FINE

Tools

Knitting tool
Tapestry needle
2 double pointed needles in
size 2 (US)

Gauge

18 sts and 20 rows to 2 in.
(5 cm) in St st (knit all rows)

Size

Shown in 8½ in (21.5 cm) foot
circumference.

Adapt

Can be adapted to any other
(smaller or larger) loom with a
peg multiple of 4.

Directions

Cast on 64 sts, join to work in
the round.

Cuff

Rnds 1–10: *k3, p1; rep from * to
the end of rnd.

Leg

Rnd 1: Knit.
Rnd 2: *k3, sl1; rep from * to the
end of rnd.
Rep rnds 1–2 until leg measures
6 in. (15 cm) from cast-on edge.
End on a rnd 2.

Open heel

Next rnd: Bind off 31 sts, knit to
the end.
Next rnd: Using the e-wrap cast
on method (see illustrated
instructions on page 11), cast on
31 sts, sl1, *k3, sl1; rep from * to
the end of rnd.

Foot

Worked in the round. Sole is worked
in St st, instep continues in the
slipped st pattern as follows:
**Next rnd: Knit.
Next rnd: k31, sl1, *k3, sl1;
rep from * to the end of rnd.**
Rep from ** to ** until item
measures 4 in. (10 cm) or desired
length from back of heel.

Toe cuff

Next 5 rnds: *k3, p1; rep from *
to the end of rnd.

Bind off

Use basic bind-off (see page 16
for illustrated instructions) to
remove loosely.

Finishing

Weave all yarn tail ends.
Block lightly.

Early dawn pedi socks option

Cuff & leg: This is worked as
yoga socks option above, but
when you reach the heel
opening follow the heel
instructions below.

Heel: Done in rows as a flat
panel using short-rows on 32
pegs. Follow short-row shaping
instructions on page 25 until 12
sts remain unwrapped. End ready
for a clockwise row. Continue
with the reverse short-row
shaping instructions on page 26.

Early dawn full length socks option

Follow instructions as for early dawn yoga socks, making the following changes to the foot.

Foot

Worked in the round. Sole is worked in St st, instep continues in the slipped st pattern as follows:

Next rnd: Knit.

Next rnd: k31, sl1, *k3, sl1; rep from * to the end of rnd.** Rep from ** to ** until item measures 7 in. (18 cm) or desired length from back of heel.

Toe option

Follow short-row shaping as previously done for the heel. Remove sts from loom as follows: Place on dpn 1: Sts from pegs 1–32.
Place on dpn 2: Sts from pegs 33–64.
Sts are now prepared to graft close. Follow grafting instructions to close the toe (see page 17 for illustrated instructions).

Finishing

Weave all yarn tail ends.
Block lightly.

Pink hottie sandal socklets

These socklets are perfect to wear with sandals so the ball of your foot stays dry and comfortable.

LEVEL 1

MATERIALS

Knitting loom

48 peg extra fine gauge knitting loom. (WonderSock loom was used in sample.)

Yarn

100 yd (90 m) of fingering weight sock yarn. (Sample uses Sweet Georgia, Superwash Sock yarn, 100% superwash merino wool, 400 yd [365 m] per 3½ oz [100 g] in Boheme.)

1 SUPER FINE

Tools

Knitting tool
Crochet hook in size 9 (US)
Stitch marker
Tapestry needle

Gauge

18 sts and 20 rows to 2 in. (5 cm) in St st (knit all rows)

Size

Shown in 8½ in (21.5 cm) foot circumference (fits up to a 9).

Adapt

Can be adapted to any other (smaller or larger) loom with a peg multiple of 4.

Directions

Cast on 48 sts, join to work in the round.

Rnds 1–4: *k2, p2; rep from * to the end of rnd.

Rnds 5–34: Knit to the end of rnd.

Rnds 35–38: *k2, p2; rep from * to the end of rnd.

Bind off

Bind off with basic bind-off method (see page 16). Cut yarn, leaving a 1-yd (1-m) tail. With yarn coming from the socklet, work 13 crochet chains. Pull yarn tail through the last loop. Count 12 sts to the right from where the chain is coming from mark this spot with a st marker. With tapestry needle seam the crochet chain at the point where the st marker is located.

Creating crochet chains

Step 1: Hold crochet hook in right hand and insert in last loop from knitted fabric.

Step 2: Bring yarn over hook from back to front and grab it with hook.

Step 3: Draw hooked yarn through slip knot and onto hook. This makes one chain st.

Repeat steps 2 and 3 in sequence as needed. One loop will always remain on hook.

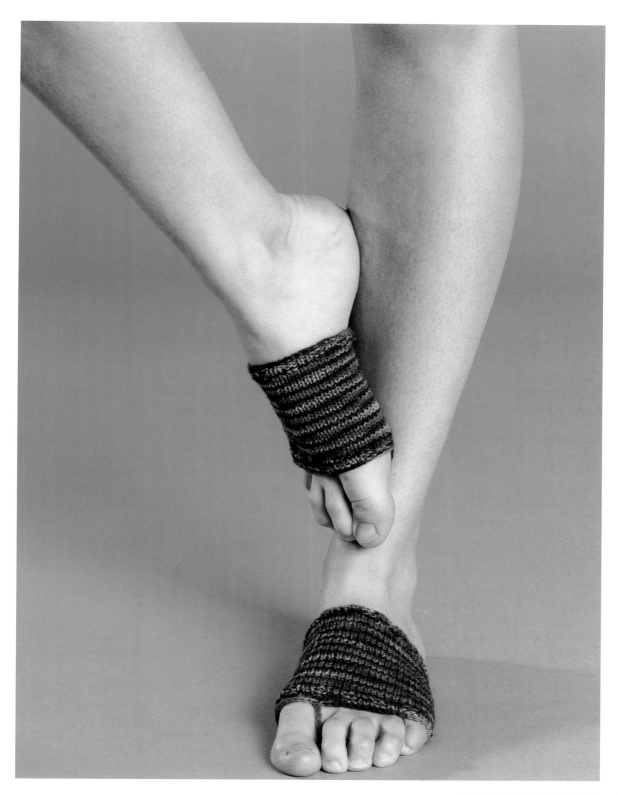

House socks

Perfect for everyone in the family these slipper socks are supersoft, warm, and you'll want to wear them to bed!

LEVEL 1

MATERIALS

Knitting loom

24 [18:14] peg large gauge knitting loom. (Pink Long Loom and Loom Clip were used in this sample.)

Yarn

90 yd (83 m) of medium weight yarn (This sample uses Berroco Plush 100% Nylon, 90 yd (83 m) per 1¾ oz [50 g].) 2 x skeins in Pink. 3 x skeins in White.

4 MEDIUM

Tools

Knitting tool 2 double pointed needles size 8 (US) Tapestry needle

Gauge

16 sts and 21 rows to 2 in. (5 cm) in St st

Sizes

To fit adult [youth: baby].

Adapt

Can be adapted to any other (smaller or larger) loom with a peg multiple of 2.

Pattern note

Knit stitch may be substituted with flat stitch or u-stitch. In the following pattern, specifics for the adult, youth, and baby patterns will look like the following:
adult [youth: baby].

Directions

Cast on 24[18:14] sts, join to work in the round.
Rnd 1–4: *k1, p1; rep from * to the end of rnd.
Rnd 5–6: Knit.

Heel shaping

Done in rows as in a flat panel using short-rows on 12[9:7] sts. Follow short-row shaping instructions on page 25 until 6[3:3]sts remain unwrapped. End ready for a clockwise row. Continue with the reverse short-row shaping instructions on page 26.

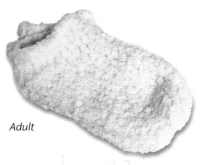

Adult

Youth

Child or baby

Foot

Work in the round until the foot measures 7[5:3] in. (18[13:8] cm) from back of heel.

Toe

Follow short-row shaping as previously done for the heel.

Child

Place on dpn 1: Sts from pegs 1–7.
Place on dpn 2: Sts from pegs 8–14.
The sts are now prepared to graft together. Follow grafting instructions to close the toe (see page 17 for illustrated instructions).

Finishing

Weave in all yarn tail ends.
Block lightly.

Bind off

Adult

Place on dpn 1: Sts from pegs 1–12.
Place on dpn 2: Sts from pegs 13–24.

Youth

Place on dpn 1: Sts from pegs 1–9.
Place on dpn 2: Sts from pegs 10–18.

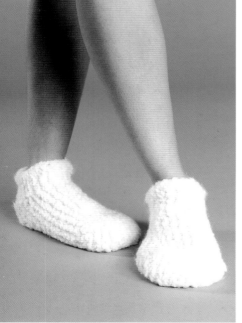

PART VII
Kids' socks

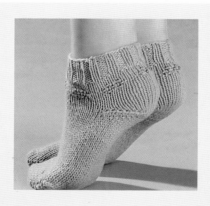

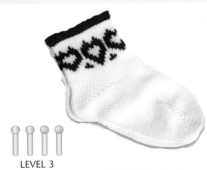

Corazoncitos (little hearts)

These socks were inspired by my daughter Nyah. She loves everything with hearts; as I was designing these, she stamped her arms, tummy, and face with hearts, inspiring this design.

LEVEL 3

MATERIALS

Knitting loom

50 peg extra fine gauge loom.

Yarn

250–300 yd (183–320 m) of sock weight yarn. (Sample uses Berroco Comfort 50% Super Fine Nylon, 50% Super Fine Acrylic 447 yd [412 m] per 3½ oz [100 g].)
1 x skein in White.
½ skein in Burgundy.

Tools

Knitting tool
Tapestry needle
2 double pointed needles size 2 (US)

Gauge

16 sts and 20 rows to 2 in. (5 cm) in St st (knit all rows)

Size

Shown in 6 in. (15 cm) foot circumference.

Abbreviations

MC is White yarn.
CC is Burgundy yarn.

Adapt

Can be adapted to any other (smaller or larger) loom with a peg multiple of 10.

Pattern note

Read chart from bottom up. Every round is read from right to left.

Stitch pattern:
Corazoncitos stitch pattern

Work from chart or follow written directions.

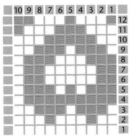

Key
CC
MC

Rnd 1: k10 MC.
Rnd 2: k2MC, k1CC, k3MC, k1 CC, k3MC.
Rnd 3: k1MC, k3CC, k1MC, k3CC, k2MC.
Rnd 4: k9CC, k1CC.
Rnd 5: k3CC, k1MC, k1CC, k1MC, K3CC, k1MC.
Rnd 6 and 7: k2CC, k5MC, k2CC, k1MC.
Rnd 8: k3CC, k1MC, k1CC, k1MC, K3CC, k1MC.
Rnd 9: k1MC, k3CC, k1MC, k3CC, k2MC.
Rnd 10: k2MC, k5CC, k3MC.
Rnd 11: k3MC, k3CC, k3MC, k1CC.
Rnd 12: k1CC, k3MC, k1CC, k3MC, k2CC.
Pattern repeat is 10 sts (only 1 vertical repeat required).

Directions

With CC, cast on 50 sts, join to work in the round.

Cuff & leg

Rnds 1–4: Knit.
Rnd 5: *k2tog, yo; rep from * to the end of rnd.
Rnds 6–9: Knit.
Rnd 10: Bring cast-on edge back to the pegs (see page 15); knit to the end of rnd. Attach MC. Do not cut CC.
Rnds 11–15: With MC knit.
Rnds 16–27: Pick up CC, and work Corazoncitos chart to the end of rnd changing colors as indicated in chart.
Cut CC leaving a 6-in. (15-cm) tail.
Rnds 28–35: With MC knit.

Heel

Done in rows as in a flat panel using short-rows on 24 sts. Follow short-row shaping instructions on page 25 until 6 sts remain unwrapped. End ready for a clockwise row. Continue with the reverse short-row shaping instructions on page 26.

Foot

Continue working in the round in St st until foot measures desired length (5 in. [13 cm] for sample) from back of heel.

Toe

Follow short-row shaping as previously done for the heel. Remove sts from loom as follows: Place on dpn 1: Sts from pegs 1–25.

Place on dpn 2: Sts from pegs 26–50.
Sts are now prepared to graft close. Follow grafting instructions to close the toe (see page 17 for illustrated instructions).

Finishing
Weave all yarn tail ends.
Block lightly.

Dress socks—for child

Matching classic socks for the little guy too. The perfect trouser sock.

LEVEL 2

MATERIALS

Knitting loom

52 peg extra fine gauge loom. (WonderSock loom was used in sample.)

Yarn

150–200 yd (137–182 m) of sock weight yarn. (Sample uses Louet Gems 100% merino wool, 185 yd [170 m] per 1¾ oz [50 g] in Pewter.)

1 SUPER FINE

Tools

Knitting tool
Tapestry needle
2 double pointed needles size 2 (US)

Gauge

18 sts and 21 rows to 2 in. (5 cm) in St st (knit all rows)

Size

Shown in 7 in. (18 cm) foot circumference.

Adapt

Can be adapted to any other (smaller or larger) loom with a peg multiple of 4.

Stitch pattern:
3x1 rib
Rnd 1: k3, p1.
Repeat this rnd for 3x1 rib.

Directions
Cast on 52 sts, join to work in the round.

Cuff & leg
Work in 3x1 rib until leg measures 5 in. (12.5 cm) from cast-on edge.

Heel
Done in rows as in a flat panel using short-rows on 27 pegs. Follow short-row shaping instructions on page 25 until 13 sts remain unwrapped. End ready for a clockwise row. Continue with the reverse short-row shaping instructions on page 26.

Foot
Worked in the round.
Next rnd: k27, p1, *k3, p1; rep from * to the end of rnd.
Repeat last rnd until foot measures 5½ in. (14 cm) from back of heel (or desired length).
Next rnd: Knit.

Toe
Follow short-row shaping as previously done for the heel, this time over 26 sts (stop the short-rowing when you have 12 sts unworked).
Remove sts from loom as follows:
Place on dpn 1: Sts from pegs 1–26.
Place on dpn 2: Sts from pegs 27–52.
Sts are now prepared to graft close. Follow grafting instructions to close the toe (see page 17 for illustrated instructions).

Finishing
Weave all yarn tail ends.
Block lightly.

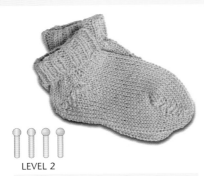

LEVEL 2

MATERIALS

Knitting loom

40 peg extra fine gauge loom. (WonderSock loom was used in sample.)

Yarn

120 yd (110 m) of fingering weight yarn. (Sample uses Louet Gems 100% merino wool, 185 yd [170 m] per 1¾ oz [50 g] in Apple Green.)

1 SUPER FINE

Tools

Knitting tool
Tapestry needle
2 double pointed needles size 2 (US)

Gauge

16 sts and 21 rows to 2 in. (5 cm) in St st (knit all rounds)

Size

6–9 months.

Adapt

Can be adapted to any other (smaller or larger) loom with a peg multiple of 4.

Cuff-down baby socks

These cuff-down baby socks are classic knits for little ones. The elastic ribbing cuff allows room and ensures that the socks will stay in place. Change the color of the cuff to make exciting outfit combinations.

Directions
Cast on 40 sts, join to work in the round.

Cuff & leg
Rnd 1–9: *k2, p2; rep from * to the end of rnd.
Rnd 10: Knit.
Rnd 11–20: *p2, k2; rep from * to the end of rnd.
Rnd 21–22: Knit.

Heel
Done in rows as in a flat panel using short-rows on 20 pegs. Follow short-row shaping instructions on page 25 until 8 sts remain unwrapped. End ready for a clockwise row. Continue with the reverse short-row shaping instructions on page 26.

Foot
Work in the round in St st until foot measures 3 in. (7.5 cm) from back of heel.

Toe
Follow short-row shaping as previously done for the heel. Remove sts from loom as follows: Place on dpn 1: Sts from pegs 1–20. Place on dpn 2: Sts from pegs 21–40.
Sts are now prepared to graft close. Follow grafting instructions to close the toe (see page 17 for illustrated instructions).

Finishing
Weave all yarn tail ends. Block lightly.

Beaded flowers child socks

Beads and little girls go great together, little beads and flowers are even better.

LEVEL 3

MATERIALS

Knitting loom

48 peg loom in extra fine gauge. (Wonder Sock Loom was used in sample.)

Yarn

150–200 yd (137–180 m) of fingering weight yarn. (Sample uses Louet Gems 100% merino wool, 185 yd [170 m] per 1¾ oz [50 g] in Champagne.)

1 SUPER FINE

Tools

Knitting tool
Tapestry needle

Gauge

15 sts and 22 rows to 2 in. (5 cm) in St st (knit all rows)

Size

Shown as 6 in. (15 cm) foot circumference.

Adapt

Can be adapted to any other (smaller or larger) loom with a peg multiple of 8.

Stitch pattern:
Flower bead

Read chart from bottom up. Every round is read from right to left. Work from chart or follow written directions.

	8	7	6	5	4	3	2	1	
				*		*			5
									4
		*		*		*			3
									2
				*		*			1

Key

☐ Knit
✱ slbd

Rnd 1: k2, bead, k1, bead, k3.
Rnd 2: Knit.
Rnd 3: k1, bead, k1, bead, k1, bead, k2.
Rnd 4: Knit.
Rnd 5: k2, bead, k1, bead, k3.

Directions

Cast on 48 sts, join to work in the round.
Rnd 1: *k2, p2; rep from * to the end of rnd.
Repeat rnd 1 until cuff measures 1 in. (2.5 cm) from cast-on edge.

Leg
Rnd 1–4: Knit.
Rnd 5–9: Work flower bead chart.
Next 4 rnds: Knit.

Heel

Done in rows as in a flat panel using short-rows on 24 pegs. Follow short-row shaping instructions on page 25 until 10 sts remain unwrapped. End ready for a clockwise row. Continue with the reverse short-row shaping instructions on page 26.

Foot

Worked in the round in St st until foot measures desired length from back of heel (4 in. [10 cm] for our sample).

Toe

Follow short-row shaping as previously done for the heel. Remove sts from loom as follows: Place on dpn 1: Sts from pegs 1–24. Place on dpn 2: Sts from pegs 25–48.
The sts are now prepared to graft together. Follow grafting instructions to close the toe (see page 17 for illustrated instructions).

Finishing

Weave in all yarn tail ends.
Block lightly.

Woven child's socks

The slipped stitches make this pattern knit up at super speed!
It works well with variegated yarns.

LEVEL 3

MATERIALS

Knitting loom

48 peg extra fine gauge loom.
(WonderSock loom was used in
sample.)

Yarn

150–200 yd (137–182 m)
of fingering weight yarn.
(Sample uses Koigu,
100% merino wool,
170 yd [155 m] per 2 oz [50 g]
in # 215.)

1 SUPER FINE

Tools

Knitting tool
Tapestry needle

Gauge

15 sts and 22 rows to 2 in.
(5 cm) in St st (knit all rows)

Adapt

Can be adapted to any other
(smaller or larger) loom with a
peg multiple of 4.

Stitch pattern:
Woven stitch

Read chart from bottom up. Every
round is read from right to left.
Work from chart or use following
instructions.

	4	3	2	1	
	⌄	⌄			4
					3
			⌄	⌄	2
					1

Key
☐ Knit
☑ slip wyif

Rnd 1: k4.
Rnd 2: (sl wyif) 2 times, k2.
Rnd 3: k4.
Rnd 4: k2 (sl wyif) 2 times.
Repeat these 4 rows for pattern.

Directions

Cast on 48 sts.

Cuff

Rnd 1: *k2, p2; rep from * to the
end of rnd.
Repeat rnd 1 until cuff measures
1 in. (2.5 cm) from cast-on edge.

Leg

Start and work in woven pattern
until leg measures 4 in. (10 cm)
from cast-on edge.
Next 4 rnds: Knit.

Heel

Done in rows as in a flat panel using
short-rows on 24 pegs. Follow
short-row shaping instructions on
page 25 until 10 sts remain
unwrapped. End ready for a

clockwise row. Continue with the
reverse short-row shaping
instructions on page 26.

Foot

Worked in the round in St st
(knit all rnds) until foot measures
desired length from back of heel
(4 in. [10 cm] for our sample).

Toe

Follow short-row shaping as
previously done for the heel.
Remove sts from loom as follows:
Place on dpn 1: Sts from pegs 1–24.
Place on dpn 2: Sts from pegs
25–48.
The sts are now prepared to graft
together. Follow grafting
instructions to close the toe (see
page 17 for illustrated instructions).

Finishing

Weave in all yarn tail ends.
Block lightly.

Fluttering socks

The butterfly pattern provides a fantastic texture to this pair—and adds a great stretching quality to the leg.

LEVEL 3

MATERIALS

Knitting loom

50 peg extra fine gauge loom. (WonderSock loom was used in sample.)

Yarn

150–200 yd (137–180 m) of fingering weight yarn. (Sample uses Sweet Georgia Yarns 100% superwash merino wool 185 yd [170 m] per 1¾ oz [50 g] in Fondant.)

1 SUPER FINE

Tools

Knitting tool
Tapestry needle

Gauge

16 sts and 23 rows to 2 in. (5 cm) in St st (knit all rows)

Adapt

Can be adapted to any other (smaller or larger) loom with a peg multiple of 10.

Stitch pattern:
Butterfly pattern

Every round is read from right to left. Work from chart or use following instructions.

10	9	8	7	6	5	4	3	2	1	
					∩					12
			∨	∨	∨	∨	∨			11
										10
			∨	∨	∨	∨	∨			9
										8
			∨	∨	∨	∨	∨			7
	∩									6
∨	∨	∨	∨	∨						5
										4
∨	∨	∨	∨	∨						3
										2
∨	∨	∨	∨	∨						1

Key

☐ Knit
☑ slip wyif
∩ Gathering loop

Rnd 1: k5, (sl wyif) 5 times.
Rnd 2: k10.
Rnd 3: k5, (sl wyif) 5 times.
Rnd 4: k10.
Rnd 5: k5, (sl wyif) 5 times.
Rnd 6: k7, gat-lp, k2.
Rnd 7: (sl wyif) 5 times, k5.
Rnd 8: k10.
Rnd 9: (sl wyif) 5 times, k5.
Rnd 10: k10.
Rnd 11: (sl wyif) 5 times, k5.
Rnd 12: k2, gat-lp, k7.

Directions

Cast on 50 sts, join to work in the round.

Cuff

Rnd 1: *k1, p1; rep from * to the end of rnd.
Repeat rnd 1 until cuff measures 1 in. (2.5 cm) from cast-on edge.

Leg

Start and work in butterfly pattern until 3 repeats have been worked.
Next 4 rnds: Knit.

Heel

Done in rows as in a flat panel using short-rows on 24 pegs. Follow short-row shaping instructions on page 25 until 10 sts remain unwrapped. End ready for a clockwise row. Continue with the reverse short-row shaping instructions on page 26.

Foot

Worked in the round in st st (knit all rnds) until foot measures 4 in. (10 cm) from back of heel (or desired length).

Toe

Follow short-row shaping as previously done for the heel. Remove sts from loom as follows:
Place on dpn 1: Sts from pegs 1–25.
Place on dpn 2: Sts from pegs 25–50.
The sts are now prepared to graft together. Follow grafting instructions to close the toe (see page 17 for illustrated instructions).

Finishing

Weave in all yarn tail ends.
Block lightly.

Abbreviations

[ ]	work instructions in brackets as many times as directed
( )	work instructions in parentheses in the place directed
* *	repeat instructions between the asterisks as directed
*	repeat instructions following the single asterisk as directed
alt	alternate
approx	approximately
bc	back cross
beg	begin/beginning
bet or btw	between
BO	bind off
c4b	a LC cable using 4 stitches
c4f	a RC cable using 4 stitches
cab	cable
CC	contrasting color
ch	chain (use a crochet hook)
cm	denotes centimeters
cn	cable needle
co	cast on
col	color
cont	continue
cr L	cross left
cr R	cross right
dbl dec	central double decrease
diam	diameter
dpn	double pointed needles
ds	double stitch
ew	e-wrap
foll	follow/following

fc	front cross
f-st	flat stitch/knit stitch
g	denotes grams
g-st	garter stitch
inc	increase
k	knit (not e-wrap)
kbl	knit through back of loop. In looming this is created by e-wrap
k2tog	knit 2 together—creates a right-slanting decrease when working with lace
k3tog	knit 3 together—creates a right slanting decrease when working with lace
l	left
lc	left cross cable (also known as ltw)
LCP	left cross purl
lp(s)	loop(s)
LTW	left twist
m	denotes meters
mb	make bobble
m1	make one—increase one stitch
MC	main color
mm	denotes millimeters
mul	multiple
oz	denotes ounces
p	purl
p2tog	purl 2 stitches together—creates a right-slanting decrease
pm	place marker
prev	previous
psso	pass slipped stitch over
rc	right cross cable (also known as rtw)
RCP	right cross purl

rem	remaining/remain
rep	repeat
rev St st	reverse stockinette stitch
rnd(s)	round(s)
rs	right side
rt	right twist
sc	single crochet
sel	selvedge
sk	skip
skn	skein
skp	slip, knit, pass stitch over—creates a decrease
sl	slip
slbd	slide bead
sl st	slip stitch
sl wyif	slip with yarn in front
ss	single stitch
ssk	slip, slip, knit these two stitches together—creates a left-slanting decrease
ssp	slip, slip, purl these two stitches together—creates a left-slanting decrease
st(s)	stitch(es)
St st	stockinette stitch (knit every row)
tog	together
tw or tw	twist stitches for a mock cable
u-st	u-stitch
wy	working yarn
yd(s)	denotes yards
yo	yarn over (e-wrap the peg)

Resources

Knitting looms

The knitting looms used in this book were provided by two vendors, Decor Accents, Inc., and Provo Craft.

Decor Accents, Inc.
P.O. Box 549
Newton, UT 84327
www.dalooms.com
admin@dalooms.com

Provo Craft
151 East 3450 North
Spanish Fork, UT 84660
www.provocraft.com

Blocking wires available from:
Take it Personally
www.giftsbytip.com

Notions

Knowknits Bags
253 West 72nd Street
Suite 1402
NYC, NY 10023
www.knowknits.com

Yarns

Berroco, Inc.
14 Elmdale Rd.
PO Box 367
Uxbridge, MA 01569
www.berroco.com
info@berroco.com

Lion Brand Yarn
135 Kero Road
Carlstadt, NJ 07072
www.lionbrand.com

Louet North America
3425 Hands Road
Prescott, ON, KOE 1TD
Canada
www.louet.com
info@louet.com

Malabrigo Yarn
8424 NW 56th St.
Ste 80496
Miami, FL 33166
www.malabrigoyarn.com
sales@malabrigoyarn.com

Shibui Knits, LLC
1101 SW Alder Street
Portland, OR 97205
www.shibuiknits.com
info@shibuiknits.com

Scout's Swag
Jamie Dixon aka Scout
Albuquerque, NM
www.scoutsswag.com
scoutj@scoutj.com

Sweet Georgia Yarns
401–228 East 4th Avenue,
Buzz 32, Vancouver, BC V5T 1G5
Canada
www.sweetgeorgiayarns.com
info@sweetgeorgiayarns.com

Index

Acknowledgments

Thank you to my wonderful husband, Sam, and my children Bryant and Nyah for their support and patience.

A multitude of thanks goes to my dear friends Bethany Dailey and Jennifer Stark for brainstorming with me through many of the book's designs and for being there through the lows and the highs of the project.

Thank you to all the loom knitters who helped knit the sample socks:

Lilly Allison, Jamie Bass, Lori Barns, Anne Bipes, Sherri Corrigan, Bethany Dailey, Karoline Filicetti, Denise Layman, Robin McCoy, Melody Mallory, Cheryl Mincey, Cindy Mott, Naomi Nova, SJ Reisner, Jennifer Stark, and Dawn VanNess.

Quintet Publishing would like to thank the models featured throughout the book: Taylor Baker, Adrian James, Danielle Holbrook, Sarah Newman, Sophie Tavendale, and Ted Tavendale.

About the author

Isela Phelps, loom knitter extraordinaire, has published several books on the subject, including the successful *Loom Knitting Primer*, and the follow up, *Loom Knitting Pattern Book*. She is an active member of the online knitting community, where she promotes loom knitting as an alternative method for creating knitted fabric. She serves as co-editor and publisher of *Loom Knitters Circle*, an online magazine for loom knitters, found at www.loomknitterscircle.com.

In her spare time, Isela enjoys hobbies such as cycling, swimming, and running. During the spring and summer months, she pedals in hundreds of miles on her road bike in support of causes such as Breast Cancer Awareness and Multiple Sclerosis.

She chronicles her loom knitting and life adventures at www.purlingsprite.com.